AJIT NAWALKHA, CO-FOUNDER OF MINDVALLEY
WITH DR. NEETA BHUSHAN

This book may be purchased for business or promotional use or for special sales.

For Information, please write to:

support@mindvalley.com Printed in the United States of America

First Printing, 2017

ISBN: 0-9993665-0-5
ISBN 13: 978-0-9993665-0-9

Mindvalley Beaverton, OR 97005-2343
www.mindvalley.com
www.evercoach.com

To my grandfather, who served humans unconditionally
and who showed me how to do the same.

And to you, the coach who cares. Deeply.

Ajit Nawalkha

For the journey of elevating human potential,
and an even better world.

Cheers, to your next chapter.

Dr. Neeta Bhushan

"If you are serious about your coaching business, read this book. You will shave off years of trial and error."

– *Christina Berkley, Leadership Coach*

"A must-read book for new and seasoned coaches."

– *Marisa Murgatroyd*
Founder and CEO, Live Your Message

"One of the simplest, most powerful books for coaches."

– *Lindsay Wilson Entrepreneur and Sales Coach*

"Ajit's astute awareness of business structures and systems is absolutely stellar!"

– *Laura Hollick*
Award-winning artist, Founder of Soul Art Studio

"Ajit is a business genius who helped me simplify my product offerings and 2x my live events in 1 year."

The late, great Psalm Isadora, Author and Sex Coach

"The best business advice I ever got in 6 years was in a single call with Ajit..."

Keith Krance
Best-Selling author "The Ultimate Guide to Facebook Advertising",
Podcast host of "Perpetual Traffic"

"Working with Ajit has been a game changer..."

Ted McGrath
Founder, Message to Millions

"Dr. Neeta is a force disrupting cutting-edge leadership, and most importantly how to build internal resilience for your businesses & organizations."

Anurag Batra
Founder/Editor-in-chief BusinessWorld India

"Combining behavioral, brain science, & positive psychology Dr. Neeta breaks it all down, making it digestible so that you can lead better for the people you serve."

– Alex Echols
Best-Selling Author, "Two Week Notice"

"Dr. Neeta shatters through the fears that business founders hide from: saving face, lack of emotional support, pretending you have it all. This is YOUR personal blackbook- from someone who's thought through your journey from the tiniest steps so that you can be triumphant."

-Emoke Vagasi
Hollywood Executive Producer

"How Dr. Neeta weaves empathy into her trainings for corporates, coaches, & organizations is what we are in most need of now. Changing the dialogue, she is the next generation for bridging the gap with her compassionate resilience."

– Regina Manzana-Sawhney
Senior Executive, Google

"Doesn't matter if you are a coach, executive, speaker, or teacher. Dr. Neeta's unique approach to teaching & asking tough questions equips you with fundamental tools applicable to succeed in any industry."

– Rohit Gandhi
Emmy Award-winning journalist & documentary filmmaker

"Ajit cuts right to the point in his coaching and teaching. I can't stress enough how important it is to work with people who've already done what you're trying to do...and Ajit has DONE it."

– Summer McStravick
Founder of M.E. School and Flowdreaming

"The combination of fearless execution & serving love that both coaches Ajit & Neeta display in this masterpiece is necessary fuel for your next chapter."

– Kute Blackson
International Speaker & Author of "You. Are. The. One"

"Ajit is not a featherweight coach. He will not necessarily tell you what you WANT to hear but he will tell you what you NEED to hear."

- Lisa Nichols
Best Selling Author, Speaker,
Founder & CEO of Motivating the Masses

CONTENTS

IGNITION

> *"We must never stop dreaming. Dreams provide nourishment for the soul, just as a meal does for the body."*
>
> -PAULO COELHO

Let me guess...

Your love affair with coaching began unexpectedly.

Maybe you hired a coach and figured; you really like the transformation you experienced.

Maybe you attended a weekend seminar or workshop, and you loved how the coach created incredible transformations and inspired the audience.

Maybe a friend became a coach and told you all about it.

No matter what your introduction to coaching, you realized one important thing: as a coach you have the power to create changes. Ripple effects that will enhance the lives of others in a big way.

The thought of serving people in this way, of doing this work, fills you with joy and excitement and now you can't imagine doing anything else

So here you are now.

Reading The Book of Coaching. Feeling curious. Wondering how to get started.

Or if you're already a coach, wondering what your next step should be. And here's the thing... You don't want to be just any coach. You want to be an *extraordinary* coach.

A coach who truly cares. A coach who's dedicated, and committed. A coach who believes in keeping promises to clients.

But there's something holding you back. It's a challenge and it's a big one.

Yes, you know what you can do. You know how much power you potentially have.

But you don't know how to tap into that power to create the changes you want to see in yourself and in your clients.

Or it could be you're a complete newbie and you're overwhelmed. What do you do first, next and after that? Where do you begin?

Plus, it's not like you haven't tried. You've been trying from day 1.

You've read the books. You've done the programs. You've attended the events. Maybe you've hired other coaches.

You've hustled. You've failed... And you've stood back up again.

I want you to know that I see you.
I hear you.
I feel you.
I know what it's like to want to make a difference but feel like you're getting nowhere.

If all of this resonates, then you're in the right place at the right time because I wrote this book for you.

The coach who has so much to give, that you wake up thinking about how to contribute more. How to create more impact and build a beautiful, abundant life and business in the process.

The coach who wants to be *extraordinary.*

This is not a book with vague theories and philosophies. It's a practical guide with specific strategies to create a thriving coaching practice now and in the years to come.

ABOUT US

I'm Ajit Nawalkha and my co-author is Dr. Neeta Bhushan. We're honored to serve as your guides - your personal coaches - throughout this book.

A little bit about me...

I'm the Co-founder of Mindvalley - a revolutionary digital education company that's changing the world.

But that's not where it all began. My story really starts in a small town in India - the ancient town of Jaipur - where I grew up with 21 other people in the house.

In India, we call it the joint family living arrangement. So you have aunts, uncles, grandparents, cousins, cousins' cousins, nieces, nephews...

Pretty much the entire extended family under one roof!

I love my family but to say that my early years were challenging is an understatement.

But I got past those years. I went way beyond what I was "*expected*" to achieve.

And it's because of the amazing people - the mentors and coaches - who showed up in my life.

I would have ended up a disillusioned engineer or an unhappy salesman with broken dreams if my mentors, teachers and coaches hadn't shown me the way to a meaningful, abundant life.

If they didn't show me what I was truly capable of.

Our greatest purpose often arises from our greatest pain and my purpose and my mission comes from my journey.

Just like my mentors and coaches showed me, I want to show others that they have greatness inside them. I want to empower them to design the kind of life they dream of.

A friend once said, *"Don't start a business. Start a mission and make it your business"*.

To me coaching is not a business. It isn't even a profession.

It's a mission to help as many coaches, healers, and teachers as I can. I want them to become the best they can be and achieve their goals and dreams.

And I know this can only happen through education. Through a learning space. A space where these amazing folks can meet, mingle, build their businesses and fine tune their craft.

I looked around and no such space existed. So I created one... And Evercoach was born.

Evercoach is a virtual hub for coaches to learn timeless methodologies as well as the latest and greatest tools and techniques to elevate their game and take their business to the next level and beyond.

Today, I'm deeply honored to say that it is the go-to digital home for a community of thousands of passionate, purposeful coaches from across the globe.

A little bit about my co –author…

Neeta is a highly sought after Emotional Health Educator and Executive Performance Coach to global leaders and CEOs as well as thousands of women from all walks of life. She's written a best-selling book called Emotional GRIT: 8 Steps to Master Your Emotions, Transform Your Thoughts and Change Your World.

Neeta's book is an in depth guide to ignite lasting transformation for anyone who wants to step into their power and become best version of themselves. From world class leaders to stay-at-home moms, Emotional GRIT is written to empower the individual so they can master their emotions, discover inner strength and revolutionize their homes, businesses and workplaces to create even more impact in the world.

Neeta is also my partner in business and in life. She is my beloved wife.

What This Book Will Do For You

This book will show you how to elevate the 3 critical elements of becoming an extraordinary coach with an extraordinary business. These 3 elements are:

You
Your Methodology
Your Business

YOU

There's a coach I know. Let's call him Jack.

Jack has been coaching for 10 years and he's successful. He makes over a quarter of a million dollars a year. He works with companies where he coaches and consults their highest level executives.

Things look perfect on the surface but there's more to it than meets the eye.

Jack's been stuck at the quarter million mark for 5, long years now. He's not having financial issues. I mean, $250,000,00 a year? No complaints, right?

But here's the thing: Jack is stuck in the vicious "dollars for hours" cycle and he doesn't know how to get past it.

This is what I call "stuck in version 1.0."

You see, like software, at different stages, we embody different "versions" of ourselves. Every time we hit a big personal breakthrough, we upgrade to a new, better version.

If you're stuck, your current version needs an upgrade.

And let me tell you a secret: there will *never* come a time when you won't need to upgrade.

You must upgrade your current version all-the-time. Constantly. It's endless.

It may sound exhausting or tiresome but it's not. It's the mark of a well- lived life.

Continuous growth and expansion. So, how does this lead back to You?

Well, all of this means that your business - and your life - cannot move forward until you do. You are the first element you need to think about when you think about your skills as a coach and business owner.

Your current "version" will define your level of success.

Your current version will define the number and quality of clients you attract. Your current version will define the impact that you have and the revenue that you generate through your coaching practice.

Higher version of yourself = higher version of clients.

Higher version of clients = better results, more impact, more income. You need to consistently create higher, better versions of yourself and this book will show you how you to do that.

YOUR METHODOLOGY

Your methodology is about how you impact your clients. How you create a transformation in their life. Your methodology includes the skills, strategies, techniques, systems and innate intelligence that you bring to your coaching sessions so your clients experience game-changing breakthroughs and amazing results.

Essentially, your methodology has to do with how you take your clients into the profound experience of transformation.

This was the area Jackie was struggling with when she came to me.

Jackie is an Intuitive Coach and she helps clients by tapping into her intuition – her gut feeling – and by helping them tap into theirs so they can come up with the solutions they need.

Jackie was great at enrolling clients. Her biggest problem? She couldn't seem to get them to come back to her, after a couple of sessions.

I worked with Jackie and found two easy solutions: create long-term coaching packages and increase prices.

Jackie did exactly that and immediately noticed a 30% boost in her revenue. She was happy.

I met Jackie again a few months later. This time she had a new problem.

Her clients were not re-enrolling even after staying with her for longer periods. Jackie couldn't understand why.

Here's the thing...

Jackie had forgotten the one rule of extraordinary coaching.

Being an extraordinary coach means continuous learning. Continuous growth. Continuous adoption and implementation of new coaching strategies you can use to up your game.

If she's serious about growing a sustainable, thriving coaching practice, Jackie needs more than a couple of coaching tools. She needs an expanding toolkit of techniques.

And so do you.

As you will discover throughout this book, you need to collect a growing set of tools you can turn to at any time so you can continue to create powerful, transformational experiences for your clients.

This book reveals a powerful set of coaching techniques, and trainings from different schools of thought that you can include as part of your unique, personal coaching methodology. The best part?

You can immediately start to use these to jumpstart your journey to becoming an extraordinary coach.

YOUR BUSINESS

Jill felt frustrated. *"I just want to help people. I know I'm a good coach. Why aren't my coaching skills enough to help me get clients?"*

Sounds like a great question, right? But it's not.

Jill's question is the same as asking, "Why isn't the world perfect? Why can't everyone wait on me hand and foot? Why don't I have a million dollars fall from the sky and into my hands?"

I know, I know. I'm exaggerating a bit but you catch my drift.

Just because you're a great coach doesn't mean you'll be a *successful* coach with a profitable practice.

Being a great coach is the first step. There are MANY more steps to becoming an extraordinary coach with an extraordinary business.

You could be the best coach in your area of expertise but that doesn't mean people will know your name.

And even if they do, it doesn't mean they'll trust you.

And it doesn't mean they've bought into the idea of trading their deepest, darkest secrets, and greatest challenges with you.

Coaching is serious stuff, people. You are moving someone through a transformation.

For someone who's going to an early grave because of poor health choices, they need to be certain their health coach can save their life.

They are risking their health with you.

For someone who's facing the end of their marriage, they need to be certain their relationship coach can save their marriage.

They are risking their happiness with you.

For someone who is desperate to grow, transform and change their life, they need to be certain their life coach can help them escape mediocrity.

They are risking their future with you.

Yes, you need to be able to do your job as coach well. Bloody well.

But you also need to know that the act of coaching is only one part of a long, trust building process that leads to success.

You also need to connect with your clients *outside* coaching sessions. You need to be at the top of their minds when they think of the challenges they have to overcome. When they think about taking their game to the next level and the next and the next.

You are the person who will transform their lives. Change everything. They need to trust you.

This book will show you how to build that trust.

When you have that trust, only then can you create a powerful, impactful business with a structure and systems that work.

Systems that allow you to work from a place of confidence and calm -not anxiety and overwhelm.

Structure and systems in your business are the building blocks that form the very foundation of an extraordinary coaching business. They create ease and efficiency and allow you to make a great living doing what you love, for a long time to come.

So, there you have it. The 3 critical elements - You. Your Methodology. Your Business.

Imagine these elements as a circular progression. You are always working on each of them to create holistic forward momentum.

This book will guide you to grow, expand and transform in all 3 elements.

How to Get the Most From This Book

Give yourself time to let everything you learn in these pages, to sink in. Reflect on the questions at the end of some of the chapters. Watch the suggested videos and talks that will help you understand new methodologies, techniques and concepts. Implement the ideas that feel right. Leave the rest. Maybe come back to them after a while and see if you feel differently.

Always remember to:

1. Keep an open mind. If you read about a tool or technique you already know, don't skip the section. Look at it with a fresh perspective.
2. Allow yourself enough time to reflect and work on the exercises and action items at the end of each chapter using the Ask Yourself section for reflection on the big ideas, as well as using the Tools as practice exercises to help you take instant action.
3. There are amazing resources, additional reading material coursework, and in depth programs to continue and deepen your learning throughout the book. Utilize them intently, and use the Resources section at the end of the book as your guide during the process. This is where the big magic happens.
4. Be patient and practice self-compassion. There's a steep learning curve ahead of you but you and your coaching practice will improve dramatically. No question.
5. Enjoy the process. Have a sense of adventure. Test out ideas and have fun!

Connect with Us: We love being in touch with our readers.

Ajit Nawalkha

https://www.facebook.com/ajitnawalkhaofficial/
https://my.linkedin.com/in/ajitnawalkha

Neeta Bhushan

https://www.facebook.com/neetabhushan1111/
https://www.linkedin.com/in/drneetabhushan/

Our Websites: To learn more about us and our work.

https://www.evercoach.com/
https://www.ajitnawalkha.com/
https://www.neetabhushan.com/

The Book of Coaching Online Experience

This book comes with a *free* online course!
This means you'll have unlimited access to hours of additional in depth, high-value training, practices, and content designed to help you fully absorb and implement the insights, techniques, systems, and ideas you've discovered in these pages.

For instance, if you want to know more about a specific concept from one of the coaches I've highlighted in the book - such as Michael Neill - the course will give you deeper insights and understanding when you listen to my full interview with him.

This unique Online Experience also includes awesome extras such as gorgeous images, photos, and videos plus it's all easily available on the web and on Android, and iOS.

When you dive into The Book of Coaching Online Experience, you'll have access to:

- Actionable, transformational training for coaches that's designed to create real world results.
- Additional strategies and proven techniques to rapidly up-level all aspects of your coaching practice.
- Tasks and exercises to skyrocket your personal and professional growth.
- A dynamic, interactive community of like-minded coaches who will share your journey and give you the support you need ... and SO much more!

Access The Book of Coaching Online Experience here:
www.evercoach.com/the-book-of-coaching/tools

Special Invite: Mindvalley Masters Community

Calling all coaches, transformational teachers, authors, experts, impact makers and anyone with a burning desire to change the world...

We'd love for you to join a growing tribe of rockstars just like you!

Become part of our private Mindvalley Masters Community here:
https://www.facebook.com/groups/mindvalleymasterscommunity/

The secret password is "Mastery" ;).

you

EPIC EXPECTATIONS

CHAPTER 1

EPIC EXPECTATIONS

> *"Remembering that I'll be dead soon is the most important tool I've ever encountered to help me make the big choices in life. Because almost everything - all external expectations, all pride, all fear of embarrassment or failure - these things just fall away in the face of death, leaving only what is truly important."*
>
> -STEVE JOBS

I was on the paradise island of Ibiza, and all I wanted to do was look out at the ocean. I wanted to take a quiet walk or maybe go to a club, dance all night and into the next morning.

But instead, I barely had time to breathe.

I was busy. Very busy. My days were completely full.

I was delivering intensives. Delivering one-on-one coaching sessions. Delivering speeches and workshops. As my friend and master coach Rich Litvin puts it, "I was coaching my ass off." If you're a practicing coach, I'm sure you can relate because you've probably experienced it yourself.

Day long sessions and you still have more to go. 10 enrollment conversations, followed by 10 more with no end in sight. Rejections from potential clients you were sure would say no. Rejections from potential clients you were sure would say yes. Feeling so motivated you think you'll never stop. Feeling so uninspired you can barely get out of bed. Moments when you want to scream your heart out because of all the pain and frustration. Moments when you want to scream your heart out because you're feeling so much gratitude and joy.

This is the life of a coach and coaches are expected to be epic. To be extraordinary. Everyone expects you to be ready to serve.

To be on a positive high. To have your tank full.
They expect you to be present and focused. To be an amazing listener.

They expect you to be: Compassionate.
Thoughtful.
Smart.
Intuitive.
Courageous.
Great in front of a camera. Great on a stage.
Great at enrolling clients. Great at re-enrolling clients.
Great at asking great questions. Great at fill-in-the-blank.

Yes, other people's expectations are high, and the list is endless but let me ask you this: is it fair to expect all of this from yourself? Sure, a few of those expectations on this list are perfectly fine. You are an extraordinary individual, after all. Unique. You care. You want to help. You want to serve.

But how are you ever supposed to live up to a bottomless vessel of other people's high expectations?

Would that be fair to you? To your clients? Would it be fair to push yourself until you have nothing left to give? Would it be fair to exploit the extraordinary level of love for humanity that you have? To stretch yourself to the breaking point?

And that's not even the biggest challenge we face as coaches.

The truth is even if others believe we're generous, kind and amazing at what we do, we never quite believe that about ourselves. No matter how much we do and how much we give, we always feel inadequate. We feel we're not good enough. We fail to hit our own epic expectations.

So, here's what you need to know now and forever.

You are good enough.

That self-deprecating inner dialogue of "not good enough" is like having an annoying Negative Nelly inside your head who never stops talking. Your inner Negative Nelly never sees the hits and focuses only on the misses. She seems like a "perfectionist" but she's just scared.

Scared of success and failure. Terrified of being visible and stepping into the spotlight. Maybe all of your negativity and lack of confidence come from being bullied as a child. Maybe someone consistently told you hurtful things about yourself, as a teenager. Maybe it was a traumatic life experience that shot your self-belief into a million pieces.

I want you to stop for a second here and take a deep breath. Let's be present in this moment so you can see yourself as you truly are.

There is a part of you that knows the truth.
You know deep down that you're capable and powerful. You know it's time to take charge and govern your life. It's time to declare you're good enough.

Heck, you're fucking great!

And here's proof: think about the roles you fulfill. Think of all that you do. You focus on growth, expansion, and improvement so you can be an extraordinary coach. You're brave enough to start a coaching practice... Or to keep it going. You work to enroll new clients. You work to re- enroll them. Maybe you speak on stages. On podcasts. On webinars. You have chosen to live the life you always wanted to live. You are taking care of your family and friends and so many others who need you.

When you break it down, you're playing many different roles

Entrepreneur.
Coach.
Growth-centered individual. Compassionate friend.
The most supportive and loving husband or wife or partner or lover you can be.
...and so many more.

Do you see what I see? I want you to give yourself a chance to appreciate what you do. I want you to give yourself a chance to set yourself free from the chains that bind you because of the impossible epic expectations you have of yourself.

So, stop. Ponder.
Stop. Wonder.
Stop. Delete some of those expectations.
Stop. Live your truth.
Stop. Know that you are enough.
And say it to yourself.
Out loud.
Again and again.

I am enough!

I was at an incredibly popular live event by Mindvalley called A-fest. It's a world class gathering of amazing folks - extraordinary entrepreneurs, artists, activists and impact makers.

At A-fest we share ideas that help us transcend our limitations and reach greater heights. It's about business. It's also about life. It's about meaning and purpose and passion and impact. We invite the best teachers on the planet to share their wisdom, and at that particular A-fest, one of the speakers happened to be Marisa Peer.

Marisa is one of the world's most respected and skilled hypnotherapists. Her client list includes royalty, celebrities such as A-List Hollywood actors and rockstars, Olympic athletes, CEOs of multibillion dollar companies and political leaders. Marisa stood on that stage at A-fest and shared openly about how some of the greatest minds we have ever known share the same "disease" as coaches do – the "I'm not enough syndrome"

It's an epidemic.

Marisa's talk at A-Fest created a worldwide movement. The global tribe who listened to her speak began to write "I am enough" all over their mirrors, walls, and even tattooed it on themselves. Marissa's talk transformed lives.

And I know it's going to transform yours.

TOOLS

I want you to take time out and watch Marisa's incredible speech. It's called The Biggest Disease Affecting Humanity:
I'm Not Enough.
Go to this link to watch the video
http://bit.ly/Iamenough

CHAPTER 2

TIME BITCH

> *"Learn to enjoy every minute of your life. Be happy now. Don't wait for something outside of yourself to make you happy in the future. Think how really precious is the time you have to spend, whether it's at work or with your family. Every minute should be enjoyed and savored."*
>
> - EARL NIGHTINGALE

I was born in India, and I grew up in a house with 22 other individuals who were constantly trying to make sense of this world; trying to make sense of the challenges around money, relationships, education and all the other aspects of being human.

When you grow up in a world like that you learn to just get by.

To survive.
To pass the time.
You don't question the norm.
You have no idea, there are such things as personal space and time.
You don't know how to be alone with yourself.

You rush to work out what's going on in your life and how you feel about things (by the way, in my childhood home, the only space and time I had to myself was in the shower! It was the only place in the house where I had a few minutes to think and process my feelings).

As you can imagine, as a boy, my personal concept of focus, of time and personal space were off balance. When I studied for my exams I never had long periods of time to myself to focus. To concentrate.

There were constant interruptions and distractions from one or more of the 21 other people in my home. I had to train my brain to operate in spurts and starts. This is what Cal Newport, Associate Professor of Georgetown University and best-selling author of Deep Work, calls "fractured time."

Fractured time is when you work in small bursts. You focus on something for a very short period before quickly moving on to something else. It's fascinating. Maybe even exciting. But it's also one of the ways to do low quality work.

Unfortunately, coaches tend to operate in fractured time. We try to be everywhere, doing everything. We feel we need to be on social media connecting with our audience and we need to be on calls connecting with clients and potential clients. We also feel we have to constantly attend seminars and workshops to upgrade our skills.

The result? Time turns into a bitch.

We're always rushing.
Always reacting.
Always responding.
We're always, asking, "I have 20 minutes between clients, what can I get done?"
It's fast.
It's hectic.
It's chaotic.
And it leads to mediocre or even poor work. So, what's the alternative?

Cal Newport has the answer.

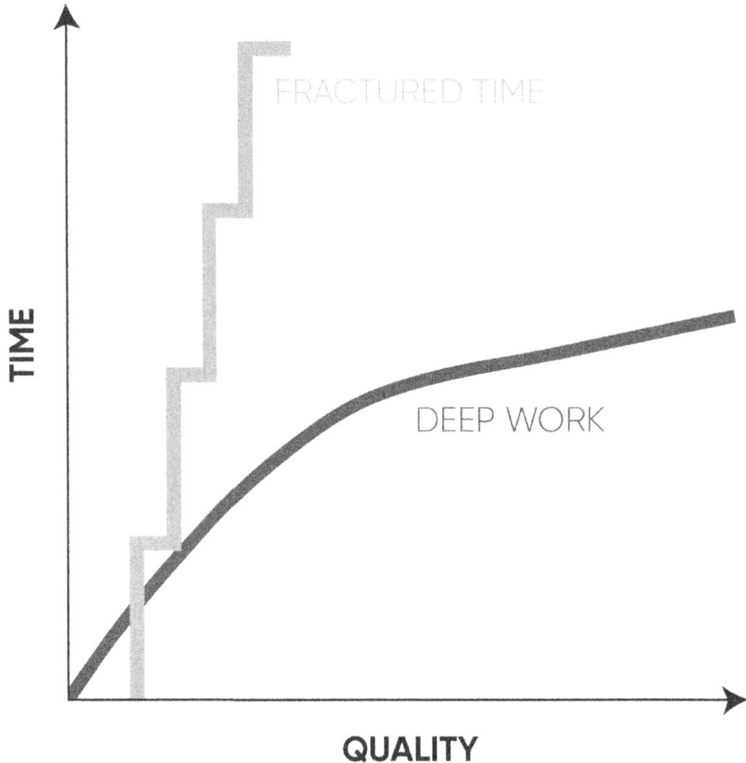

Deep Work Mode

Deep work happens when you get to have a period of uninterrupted time to focus on a single task or activity. Successful intellectuals do their best work when they go into isolation and get into deep work mode.

Carl Jung wrote some of his greatest theories working and thinking in isolation, and he became one of the greatest psychologists of all time. Modern day intellectuals, such as leading expert in motivation, Adam Grant, is also known to work in isolation. Deep work helped him write his New York Times best-sellers Give and Take and Originals.

You may argue that entrepreneurs - no matter how successful - don't do deep work and you'd be right. An entrepreneur's role is that of an executive, who mainly responds to data, situations around them, and then makes decisions.

But coaches need to operate in the same way as an intellectual. Coaching requires intense periods of focus and concentration.

You need to be able to ask your clients brave questions at the right time.

You need to be able to connect with your clients and get them to see what they need to see so they can hit their goals.

You need to be able to share thought-provoking stories and metaphors to drive home a point. And you have to come up with these stories in seconds.

Coaching is a refined, intellectual craft, and it needs deep work.

Fractured Time Mode

But then coaches are also entrepreneurs. They need to enroll clients. They need to work on administrative tasks like billing and agreements. They need to post on social media.

Make calls.
Go to events.
React.
Respond.

My incredibly successful business partner, Vishen Lakhiani, works mainly in fractured time mode. He likes to work with other people in an open concept office space. Co-author of this book, and one of the most extraordinary coaches I know, Neeta Bhushan, operates mainly in deep work mode.

Neeta is outstanding at running group coaching calls and has written an amazing best-selling book called *Emotional GRIT: 8 ways to Master Your Emotions, Transform Your Thoughts, & Change Your World.* Vishen runs Mindvalley - the multi-million dollar educational company and has also written a best-seller called *The Code of The Extraordinary Mind.*

So, what the heck are we supposed to do here? Which one's better? Fractured time mode or deep work mode?

The answer is both.

They fit together like the yin and yang symbol. These two modes of operation are great alone, but together, you're looking at a powerhouse pair.

To illustrate what I mean, let's go back to Adam Grant. Grant, segments his year into two main chunks. In one chunk he goes into deep work mode and does a lot of research. He writes his papers and produces his outstanding books during this time.

In the other part of the year, Grant spends his days at Wharton. He is the youngest full tenure professor at this prestigious school and also one of the highest rated teachers there. At Wharton, Grant experiences the everyday routine and responsibilities of a teacher. Handling his students' questions and concerns, leading classes, attending faculty meetings and all the rest. He's mostly in fractured time mode.

Grant's deep work mode, helps him operate in fractured time mode. He spends a solid chunk of time writing. Then he spends a solid chunk of time teaching. Knowing how to separate the two allows him to be amazing at both.

Deep work facilitates fractured time work.

When you are in fractured time mode, you are mainly responding to external cues. This is great for communication and decision making. You need to do this well if you want to be a successful entrepreneur. But also need to be a phenomenal coach, and that can happen only when you are in deep work mode.

So, get into deep work when you're with a client. When you want to learn new coaching methodologies and techniques. When you want to write and research. Then come up for air so you can respond and react quickly and accurately as an entrepreneur in fractured time.

Get into deep work to achieve blissful fractured time work.

Ask Yourself

"How can I schedule my time in a way where I can go deep every, single week? Maybe even take an entire month to get into deep work mode? How can I find different ways to create space for deep work on a regular basis? What would that look like?"

TOOLS

#1 Most coaches don't take the time to pick a calendar and schedule activities. Take an excel sheet. Mark the Columns as months and Rows as weeks. Then schedule your tasks for every week so you can live a life filled with deep work.

#2 Cal Newport's book Deep Work will help you to understand this topic a lot more. Plus, it's a great read! You can find the book here: http://bit.ly/Deep-Work

CHAPTER 3

DRIVE

> *"Motivation will almost always beat mere talent."*
>
> -Norman Ralph Augustine

Sometimes, I start a brand, new project with a ton of energy and enthusiasm but then it fizzles out. I lose my motivation. My drive. This could happen with any project – prospecting clients, creating a new marketing campaign, and even writing this book. When I checked with friends, entrepreneurs, and other coaches, I discovered they've all felt this way at one time or another.

As you may know, I come from humble beginnings in India. Tiny house. Very little money. I suppose it was only natural that I felt money had a lot of power. That it would solve everything.

At the start of my working life, it was all about the money. My income defined my career. It controlled everything. What I did and how hard I worked were directly related to how much money I could make.

But I couldn't find a lasting sense of fulfillment, joy or freedom.

I call this the "More Money Conundrum." Going all out for more money motivates you to start out with a bang, but eventually, you lose your drive. The More Money Conundrum is a major challenge, and thousands of coaches grapple with it every day. Using money as your only motivator to keep doing extraordinary work and to keep hitting extraordinary goals, just doesn't work.

So, I decided to dig deeper and find out what truly motivates people. My research led me to 2 key questions:

1. How do we lose our motivation?
2. How can we stay in a state of flow, high performance, and high drive?

The answers I uncovered were interesting. Complex enough that they could fill an entire book, but I'm going to attempt to unravel and explain it concisely here so you'll know what motivates you, and what demotivates you. I'll also share how you can achieve a state of flow for consistent high performance.

Let's begin with the motivation piece.

The Puzzle of Motivation

Dan Pink is one of the world's greatest thought leaders and he's invested a considerable amount of time and effort in understanding motivation. He conducts experiments on this subject, but one of the most interesting studies he refers to isn't one of his own. He talks about it in his 2009 TED talk called The Puzzle of Motivation. This study was carried out by economist Dan Ariely.

Many of us believe money is our biggest motivator. You think money will ignite your drive and persistence. Well, Dan Ariely can prove you wrong.

Here's part of the transcript of Pink's talk:

"Dan Ariely is one of the great economists of our time. He and 3 colleagues did a study of some MIT students. They gave these MIT students a bunch of games that involved creativity, motor skills, and concentration. Then he offered them, for performance, three levels of rewards: small reward, medium reward, large reward. If you do really well, you get the large reward, on down.

What happened? As long as the task involved only mechanical skills, bonuses worked as would be expected: the higher the pay, the better the performance. Okay? But once the task called for even rudimentary cognitive skill, a larger reward led to poorer performance.

Then, they said, "Let's see if there's any cultural bias here. Let's go to Madurai, India and test it." The standard of living is lower. In Madurai, a reward that is modest by North American standards, is more meaningful there. Same deal. A bunch of games, three levels of rewards.

What happens? People offered the medium level of rewards did no better than people offered the small rewards. But this time, people offered the highest rewards, did the worst of all. In eight of the nine tasks we examined across three experiments, higher incentives led to worse performance."

Later in his talk, Pink shares an insight that sheds light on the truth about motivation:

"...There is a mismatch between what science knows and what businesses do. Here is what science knows.

One: Those 20th century rewards, those motivators we think are a natural part of business, do work, but only in a surprisingly narrow band of circumstances.

Two: Those if-then rewards often destroy creativity.

Three: The secret to high performance aren't rewards and punishments, but unseen intrinsic drive - the drive to do things for their own sake. The drive to do things because they matter."

The drive to do things for their own sake.
The drive to do things because they matter.

The old definition of success being tied only to money, screws with what's truly important to us. If you feel challenged or demotivated, could it be because you're connecting your level of motivation to the "rewards" you receive? Could it be because you have connected your success to things that don't really matter? As I started to understand motivation, I began to see why I was failing at staying motivated.

Here's the cycle that I was often trapped in:

- I connected my success as a coach to how much revenue I generated.
- I compared myself with other coaches who were sometimes further ahead in their journey and felt demotivated about where I was.
- I was in the carrot and stick system where I allowed myself to feel like a winner only if I hit massive goals, first.

Do you see some of these issues showing up in your life? These are the reasons why you could be dealing with a disturbing lack of motivation. That's what Ariely discovered and what Pink meant when he said extrinsic motivators - like monetary rewards - only work for mechanical, rudimentary tasks. For high level, cognitive, creative work like coaching, extrinsic motivators will hinder your progress. It can even lead to low performance.

What does this mean for you? To stay motivated, turn to intrinsic motivators – those things you do because you love to do them. You love coaching. That's why you do it. It's the only motivational tool you need.

But let's not stop here.

Being in Flow

Studies have found that when you love doing something, you welcome challenges. This is because you are happy to build the skills you need, to overcome those challenges.
Take a moment to take that in.

When your skills match the love you have for the task at hand, you actually enjoy challenges.

That's when true magic happens. That's when you create your best work. That's when flow happens.

When you enter a state of flow you achieve the perfect balance between challenge and skill. If what you're doing is too easy, you'll get bored. If it's too hard, you'll feel anxious. It's got to be just right. The perfect balance between challenge and skill.

Having a worthy challenge and intrinsic motivators will keep you on the field of play long after everyone else has given up and gone home. It will create flow, and joy, and fulfillment. It's the secret to lasting motivation...

And endless drive.

Ask Yourself

What motivates me? What holds me back? Why do I lose my drive? What keeps me going no matter what?

TOOLS

#1 Below is a grid I call the Anxiety/Boredom Identifier. This grid will help you discover if you're anxious or bored. It can also help change your state and enter into a flow state more often.

Goal/ Skill	Skill 1	Skill 2	Skill 3	Skill 4	Skill 5	Skill 6	Skill 7
Goal 1							
Rating (1-5)							
Goal 2							
Rating (1-5)							

First write down your goals. Then rate the skills you need to use to achieve each goal. If you rate your skill level as 5, you are probably overqualified for the challenge or goal. This means you're going to feel bored and demotivated. If you give yourself a 1, you are probably anxious. Look for the sweet spot of a rating of 3 or 4.

#2 To dive deeper into the fascinating topics of motivation and flow read books by Daniel Pink and Mihaly Csikszentmihalyi.

CHAPTER 4

BEWARE OF FALSE LEGENDS

> *"Believe what your heart tells you, not what others say."*
>
> -UNKNOWN

Seth Godin wrote a book called, "All Marketers Tell Stories." It was previously called "All Marketers are Liars." To some degree, both statements are true.

Most marketers are good at telling and positioning stories - true stories or pure fiction - so they catch on like wildfire through channels of communication such as social media platforms. Most of us find it almost impossible to tell the difference between fact and fiction in these marketing campaigns.

And this is what False Legends in coaching and in other industries - rely on. They make up stories knowing it's hard to differentiate fiction from fact. They are usually great presenters. Genius communicators. They have the power to get you to believe something that's completely untrue.

They appear to have it all. They achieve incredible overnight success. They say they have organically expanded their fan base - minus advertising and marketing. Their sales numbers are astronomical. Everything they touch turns to gold.

And what ends up happening is you feel like failure in comparison.

You feel lost.

Overwhelmed.
Left behind.

You might even quit your coaching practice because you're measuring your success against stories that aren't even true. This is a tragedy that I see it happen way too often.

I want you to avoid this and you can do it when you learn to identify the False Legends around you.

The Significance Junkie

I used to be in a group that included a few False Legends. They would attend group meetings, get bottle service, drive expensive cars and share "game-changing business secrets."

I was fascinated.
Captivated.
I tried their ideas, and I fell flat on my face. But I was ok with that.
It's business.
Some things work. Some don't.

But it didn't end there.

At the next meeting, they would share a new "truth." A new "secret." It baffled me that they were so calm when each "secret" didn't work and how they always, conveniently, had a new "secret" to replace the old one.

See, these individuals aren't legends but ordinary folks looking for significance. They were hoping to be accepted and loved. That's the first type of False Legend. The ones who are always looking for meaning and significance.

Then there's the other type of False Legends - the ones who claim they found the proverbial pot of gold at the end of the rainbow.

The Overnight Success

"I started my business, and 7 days later I made 100,000 bucks..."

This type of False Legend claims to be an overnight success, but no one can claim that because there's no such thing as an overnight success. Journalist, speaker, and best-selling author Malcolm Gladwell, wrote about how it takes 10,000 hours to become an expert at anything.

But experts have found the 10,000-hour rule is only half true.
It takes more than 10,000 hours to be an expert.
It takes deliberate practice.
It takes a feedback loop and much, much more.

When False Legends talk about their overnight successes, they are either lying, or they are ignoring the amount of preparation that went into achieving success.

I know a coach who lives in Silicon Valley. Let's call him Jason. In his first year, Jason clocked 6-figures with his coaching practice. Jason doesn't talk about his success. He's modest. But when people ask, he shares his story of hitting 6-figures in his first year of coaching.

What Jason forgets to share is this:

He founded two tech companies before becoming a coach. He sold those companies and enjoyed great profits. He was already known as an entrepreneur before he became a coach. He knew a lot of people and a lot of people respected him in The Valley He enrolled clients easily because he reached out to people who liked and admired him as an entrepreneur. So, when he informed them he was now a coach, they asked, "Where do I sign?"

There are many other "Jasons" whose successes may cause you to feel envious. It's not because these "Jasons" have some special power that you don't or that they're better than you.

They're just ahead of you in their journey.

They were doing the work to reach success without even realizing it. They were building trust long before they were aware of it...

Look up to the "Jasons" of the world if you want to. Learn from them. But don't be envious. Don't compare. Don't feel unworthy.

Because you're not.

Ask Yourself

"Are people who achieve outstanding success truly who they say they are? What is their back story? Are their stories a little outrageous? Do their stories make sense? Do they match their journey? What is it about them – what part of their character – can I emulate? What is it that I can learn from them? What should I avoid?"

TOOLS

Identifying False Legends

This activity will help you identify False Legends in your life, and the times you may have felt like one yourself. Doing this will help you shine a light on your authentic skills and chart your path to success

1. *Can you recall a time when you met a False Legend? What did you learn from this experience?*
2. *Was there ever a time when you felt like a fraud or a False Legend yourself? What do you need to change so this doesn't happen again?*
3. *Reflect on where you were 3 years ago. Who were you then? Who are you now? What are the skills and that has brought you to this point in your life?*
4. *What other skills have you accumulated areas other than coaching? You may take these skills for granted but everything you learn can be used to help you create success in your current path to becoming extraordinary coach.*

THE CENTERPIECE

CHAPTER 5

THE CENTERPIECE

> *"Let him who would move the world first move himself."*
>
> \- SOCRATES

The pressure was on.

We had recently experienced a massive growth spurt in the company, and we were up against some major changes that could potentially make or break us.

It was now or never. Go time.

And then, out of nowhere, a curve ball hit. Our rockstar marketing expert was offered an exciting new opportunity and decided to move on. I was conflicted. Should I let her go so she could her pursue her passion? Should I be selfish and entice her to stay with the company? Maybe offer an irresistible incentive that would get her to stick around?

What do I do?

If I let her go, I'd have to do all of the work myself. I had trained her personally, and I'd shared everything I knew about marketing. I'd passed on my knowledge so I could finally have some time to focus on long-term projects that would lead to company-wide expansion. Now it was all going to go to hell in a handbasket. I wrestled with my options for a few days, and then I did what I knew was right.

I let love win.

It would mean temporary pain, some upheaval, and chaos on our side but love had to win. I let her go and wished her well. She soon found a project she was fired up about and discovered talent she didn't even know she had. She found her purpose. She loved her new gig. And she never looked back.

As for us, everything turned out fine. We moved forward. Created new structures. New systems and workflow. We didn't even need to hire a new marketing expert to replace our rockstar. Somehow, it all worked out. That wasn't the first time I'd experienced things falling into place without any effort on my part. And it definitely wasn't the last time.

We attach so much of our business success to external situations and other people that we forget the most important thing of all: as long as the centerpiece is in good standing, things will always work out.

What's the centerpiece?

The centerpiece changes depending on the size of a company or business. Sometimes it's a team that shows up as a centerpiece. In this book and for our conversation here, we're going to focus on coaching businesses run by a solopreneur or those with smaller teams, and this means the centerpiece is the business owner.

This means the centerpiece is YOU.

Work On the Centerpiece

Your growth as an individual defines the growth of your business. Your ability to go deep with yourself allows you to go deep with your work as a coach. Your courage translates to fearlessness in your coaching. Your ability to have extraordinary conversations leads to extraordinary results for clients. Your power to get past your negative beliefs, limiting inner dialogues, and disempowering stories from your past, ignites your clients' power to get past negative beliefs, limiting inner dialogues, and disempowering stories from their past.

You are the centerpiece.

I love interacting with coaches during live events like the Evercoach Summit where we hone in on the key pillars to build a thriving coaching practice. We discuss things like daily routines, branding, message, and purpose. The only problem? I've found that with most coaches, these pillars do not focus on the coach as the centerpiece.

Instead, these key pillars seem to be client-centered. Or sales-centered. Or delivery-centered.

And it's because of one thing: fear.

In Disguise

Sometimes it's the fear of money. Or lack of money.
Sometimes it's the fear of being alone.
Sometimes it's the fear of emptiness.
Sometimes it's the fear of not being significant.
Sometimes it's the fear of not being loved.

These fears are sneaky. They don't show up as fear. They show up disguised as "I have to work hard," "I have to grow and expand," "My business needs to make X dollars to be a success."

Push. Hustle. These are now synonyms for coaches not wanting to deal with their fear. We bury our fears by working all the time. We do our best not deal with them. I won't lie. Hiding fears and working nonstop can create results. For some people.

But not for coaches and here's why.

Coaches don't get to hide their feelings and bury their emotions.

You can't hide because what you do for a living - your purpose as a coach – is to help people to step up and step out.

To help them transform.

To change their world. To NOT hide.

You can't help them stand strong; you can't help them discover their power, their purpose, their drive if you haven't done that yourself.

You can't be the coach you are meant to be if you don't do the work and face your fears. You want an extraordinary business and extraordinary clients? Work on yourself until you're an extraordinary coach.

You want consistent, high income months in your coaching practice? Work on yourself until you can generate and sustain that level of income.

You want to have a greater impact on the world?

Work on yourself until you can do what it takes to create greater impact.

Work hard to overcome your fears. Keep going for your highest potential.

Because you are the force that drives it all - your business, your team, your clients.

You are the centerpiece.

TOOLS

You as the centerpiece of your business is a powerful, game-changing concept and one that my dear friend and best-selling author of Prison Break, Jason Goldberg, often refers to as self-leadership. Jason regularly shares priceless insights and strategies on how you can lead yourself to the highest levels of success. One of the best talks he's ever given on the subject was at our Evercoach Summit.

Click here to watch the power-packed video of Jason's talk or go to this link: http://bit.ly/Self-Leadership.

CHAPTER 6

BECOMING EXTRAORDINARY

> *"The ordinary are here to fit into the world; the extraordinary are here to create their own worlds."*
>
> -Matshona Dhliwayo

When we learn what being extraordinary is about – the things we must think and feel and do - we will know how to become extraordinary. My business partner, Vishen Lakhiani, wrote an entire book about this in 2016. It's called, *The Code of the Extraordinary Mind.*

Vishen is an engineer by qualification, and he's all about finding fast, effective solutions to complex problems. This is the reason he absolutely loves the concept of "hacking." Vishen is passionate about hacking just about everything and let me just say that when it comes to living an extraordinary life, Vishen achieved what he set out to do. He discovered how to hack being extraordinary.

After discussing the concept with over 200 experts in scores of related fields, he found that the path to becoming extraordinary involves continuous evolution through 4 different levels.

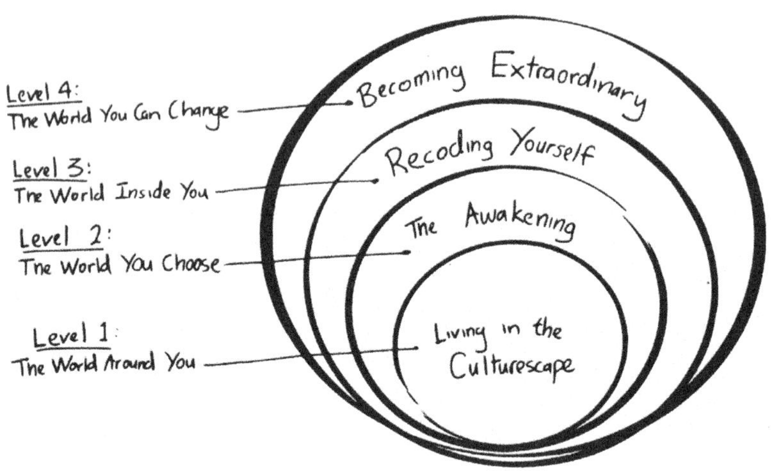

[Image from the book: The Code of the Extraordinary Mind, Know more here: http://www.thecodexmind.com/]

Integrated within these 4 levels of evolution, Vishen reveals 10 rules you need to follow to become extraordinary.

Rule #1 Transcend the Culturescape

Our culturescape dictates the rules of engagement in life and business. These are rules and ideas that have been passed down from generation to generation, over decades and centuries. These rules and ideas have been around for a long time.

And these rules and ideas are wrong.

As Vishen puts in in his book, these are not truths but *relative truths*. I can tell you with pretty much 100% certainty that believing and operating from the culturescape that you were born into, that you grew up in, or currently live and work in, is limiting what's possible for you.

If we are to live extraordinary lives, we must question the culturescape we live in and the rules it holds up. Do we really agree with those relative truths? Are they right for us?

When I was growing up, my culturescape included being a Jain (a religion that's similar to Buddhism). Being a Jain carried a lot of relative truths. Other religions aren't as good as Jainism. Jains are extra special. We are blessed to be born as Jains.

What has your culturescape taught you? What are the relative truths hidden within? Do you still want to believe in them? Are you willing to transcend them?

Rule #2 Question The Brules

Brules is an acronym for "Bullshit Rules." Brules exist because we are told to follow rules that were laid out by others. Rules that are not necessarily right for us.

There are Brules for doing just about everything.

There are Brules for working.
Brules for loving.
Brules for existing.
Brules for everything.

Are the Brules serving you? Or are they limiting you? Are those Brules designed to help you, or they are designed to limit you, so you don't disrupt or change the status quo for everyone else?

I was born in India. Today, this doesn't hold me back or stop me from going for my dreams. Why should it? But when I first started Evercoach it was one of the Brules that was implanted in me by someone I know. They did it without meaning to, I know, but the impact of it was real and long lasting.

This person told me I have a distinct Indian accent (which I do). He said no one would let me speak on stage. No one would hire me to coach them. No one would pay any attention to me because of my accent. It sounds ridiculous to me now, and as it turned out, none of it was true, but for a considerable amount of time, I believed it.

Then there's the other Brule I was told: you have to be a white female to get ahead as a coach. When I think about this today, it's funny, but it wasn't so funny back then. I remember when I shared my idea about Evercoach with a few movers and shakers in the coaching industry. The first thing they said? "Well, if you were a white female, it would work."

I decided enough was enough. It was time to call a spade a spade. It was time to call a Brule a Brule. Light dawned only when I realized how this rule about being a white female coach was complete B.S. I saw that their thinking was very limited. I saw that I had bought into a couple of Brules and stopped myself from reaching further and higher. I had dimmed my light.

Don't let Brules stop you. Make it your job to identify them. To question them. To challenge them. And then, to rewrite them.

Rule #3 Practice Consciousness Engineering

Consciousness Engineering is a powerful method to hack your beliefs and habits. It's a framework for understanding how your beliefs and practices shape who you are.

There are two parts to this.

Models of Reality: These are your beliefs, and... Systems for Living: These are your habits and practices.

Consciousness Engineering suggests that you can dissect and categorize your life and how you operate into a set of beliefs. If you believe coaching is hard, it will be hard for you. But it's just your belief. There are individuals who believe coaching is easy and it's easy for them.

The Model of Reality becomes embedded in your mind and your life because your habits and practices – your Systems for Living - keep it alive. If coaching is hard for you, it's because you're using the same strategies to enroll people. Strategies that are not working. It's your habit. Your practice. If you want to change your Model of Reality, you have to learn from individuals who have a model that is very different from yours and who use Systems of Living that are very different from yours.

So, if you think coaching is hard, find someone who thinks it's easy. Learn from their practices and habits. You can then adapt their Model of Reality and Systems for Living so they work *for you.*

Rule #4 Rewrite Your Models of Reality

These are the beliefs ingrained in you since you were a child. Many are disempowering and keep you stuck in problematic, painful, or mediocre ways of being in the world. Think hard about the Models of Reality that you have been following. Are they serving you or are they limiting you?

Rule #5 Upgrade Your Systems for Living

Your Systems for Living are your daily practices for getting on with life. These Systems include everything from eating to working to coaching to enrolling clients to parenting to making love. New Systems for Living are being discovered all the time. Most just never make it into our formal education system. So, most of us learn, love, work, practice spirituality, and parent using models that are suboptimal or even damaging.

You can upgrade your Systems for Living by finding new ones and testing them. Testing Systems has led me to be in the best shape of my life, while living a purposeful, fulfilling existence. I must warn you that you will fail when you try to change old habits for new ones - but only at first. Stick to it, and you will find the best Systems for yourself. I promise you; it's worth the effort.

Rule #6 Bend Reality

There is an optimal state of living where everything seems to click, and luck seems to be something you can control. I've met many remarkable people who appear to exist in this state.

Some are monks. Some are billionaires.

This phenomenon can be explained with this simple quote by Vishen, "Have big goals—but don't tie your happiness to your goals. You must be happy before you attain them."
It's that delicate balance that you need to have, so you can feel happiness in the now, and still maintain a vision of the future that will drive you forward. Being in this state will create so much power that it will feel like the Universe is operating just for you.

Rule #7 Live in Blissipline

Happiness is hackable, and Blissipline is a beautiful discipline for leveling up your happiness every day. Creating bliss in every moment is not as complicated as you might imagine. There are 3 principles that you can practice on a daily basis that will boost your happiness and bliss levels.

These principles are gratitude, forgiveness, and giving.

Gratitude
What are you grateful for today? Now? It doesn't have to be something big. It can be something small and inconsequential but know that it matters. Your contribution to the world matters. Your ability to do what you do matters. Always.

Forgiveness
This one's hard to do, but when you forgive someone for hurting you in any way, it sheds dead weight from your soul. You rise. You feel light. You are free again. Give yourself this gift.

Giving
The act of giving something to someone in need, or giving for no reason, giving *just because*, will give you amazing amounts of joy.

What can you express gratitude for now? Who do you need to forgive now? What can you freely give to someone in need, now?

Rule #8 Create a Vision for Your Future

Most of us have been trained by the Brules of the world to pursue the wrong goals and I've seen this happen again and again with coaches. Our work and our service seem to tie to our bank accounts.

But here's the truth...

We don't experience money. We experience what money can do for us. So, instead of asking, how much income you'll make this year, how about we ask a different set of questions? How about we ask:

What experiences I do I want to have? How do I want to grow as a human being? What is my contribution to the world?

Asking these questions expands how you view life. It allows you to reimagine your goals.

Rule #9 Be Unf*ckwithable

What can you do so you're rock solid within yourself? What can you do so judgments from others or fear of loss no longer affect you? You need to be unshakeable in your journey through the world. Living at your highest potential and changing the world are not easy goals. They're tough. Find ways to become strong enough to weather the storm.

Rule #10 Embrace Your Quest

And then there's rule number 10. Here you learn to go beyond just living in the world to changing it by discovering your quest. When you find it - and you may have already found it - you take that final step and embrace that quest. Make it a part of who you are so you can start living an extraordinary life.

Some of these 10 rules may apply to you. Some may not. That's ok. There is no linear structure to becoming extraordinary. These rules are meant to work as a rough guide for you to question what is...

So, you can start to create what can be.

TOOLS

If you don't already own a copy of The Code of the Extraordinary Mind, go to this link: http://www.thecodexmind.com/. It's an outstanding book that you want to keep handy. It contains simple, powerful, implementable tools you can use in your personal life and tools you can use to coach your clients.

CHAPTER 7

REDEFINING GOALS

"It's not about the goal. It's about growing to become the person that can accomplish that goal."

-Tony Robbins

There was a time when I attached my self-worth to my bank account. If the numbers were good, I felt worthy. If the numbers were low, I felt unworthy.

This also meant I had some pretty outrageous goals. I would set an insane income goal. Then, I'd motivate everyone to get behind it. I'd work like there was no tomorrow. Sometimes I would hit the goal. Sometimes, I would miss. I thought that was the only way to do it. Set unbelievable goals and go for it with everything you have.

Then, I found another way. A better way.

As I learned more and experienced more, I realized that having a goal defined by money gave me short-term gratification but failed to give me long-term fulfillment. It failed to keep me happy and producing great work that I loved. Work that made me proud.

So, I went back to the beginning and looked at how goals are defined.

The 12 Categories

It turns out, goals are a function of: Our past experiences
Our vision of ourselves

Our past experiences frame what is possible and what is not. What we can do, and what we can't do. Our vision of ourselves is that perfect self that we create in our minds about who we must become and what we must have. 6-pack abs. Millions in the bank. Beach villa. Trips around the world.

You can achieve just about any goal with enough time and effort. But what ends up happening is that we bring these long-term goals into our immediate future. We try to achieve massive goals in just 6 months or even 3 months.

Let's launch this product and make a million dollars next week. Let's get on this diet and lose all the extra weight in 10 days.

Setting a goal with such a tight timeframe leads to frustration and anxiety. This isn't going to help you achieve that goal.

So, what's the trick to effective goal setting? How do you redefine it goals so you can actually achieve them?

First, never create a short-term goal if you can help it. Short- term goals, lead to short-term outcomes, which lead to in-the-moment gratification that disappears as quickly as it arises.
This is not the road to long-term success.

Instead, start by creating a vision for your far out future. Something that you can capture and hold in your imagination. Something that feels deeply aligned with your values. I use the 12-Lifebook categories to craft my goals and my vision.

Lifebook is a transformational life development experience founded by Jon and Missy Butcher. They are among the most loving, kind and successful entrepreneurs I've ever had the privilege to meet.

They first created the Lifebook system because they wanted a powerful way to capture their own life vision.

Here are the 12-Lifebook categories Jon and Missy identified:

1. Your Health and Fitness
2. Your Intellectual Life
3. Your Emotional Life
4. Your Character
5. Your Spiritual Life
6. Your Love Relationship
7. Parenting
8. Your Social Life
9. Your Financial Life
10. Your Career
11. Your Quality of Life
12. Your Life Vision

Here's something fascinating that I observed when I worked on these 12 categories. I looked at my current goals, and most of my goals were in just 4 areas:

Career, Health, Financial, and Relationships.

This is true for most people. We focus on just a few areas of our life and neglect all the others. Life is a great adventure, and the world is full of limitless possibilities. There is so much to explore and to know and so many kinds of goals and dreams that will bring you happiness and fulfillment. To confine yourself to just a few categories is to cheat yourself from experiencing joy.

So, here's what I want you to do right now. Grab a paper journal or digital notebook and list the 12 categories. *Then imagine your ideal self and what you would like your life in each of the 12 areas. Write down your thoughts next to each category.*

When you're done, you're ready to redefine your goals. I've found that goals that are set 3-years out are ideal. 5 years is too long and 1 year is too short.

The idea is to give yourself a realistic amount of time to achieve the goal. Realistic here means the goal is far enough away for you to pursue it without constant anxiety and frustration but it's close enough for you to feel like you need to start taking action now.

When you've set your 3-year vision, go ahead and map out what needs to happen each year for you to achieve that 3-year vision. This method makes so much more sense than arbitrarily creating 1-year goals.

Now you have something juicy to aim for at the end of 3 years and something that's juicy this year, next year and the following year, that will help you bring your 3-year vision to reality. This way, the vision is big enough, but it's chewable. It leaves space for bliss and joy.

But you're not done yet.

When you have your yearly goal extracted from your 3-year vision, chunk it down further.

What needs to happen every month, over the next 12 months? What needs to happen each week of those 12 months?

Chunking down your goals makes them real. Plus, it gives you clarity. Now you know what needs to be achieved every week.

Every day.

Now you can tie your life vision to your daily work, play, relationships; anything and everything. Now your actions will feel aligned because your actions are aligned.

TOOLS

#1 Here is an exercise that will get you started on redefining your life goals in the 12 categories. It's called the 3 Most Important Questions to Ask Yourself. Answer these 3 questions for each of the 12 categories mentioned above. Follow this link and do this exercise
http://www.mindvalley.com/goal-setting-redefined

#2 Here is a helpful grid called the Redefined Goals Grid, to help you break down your 3-year vision into chewable bites. This is the first part of the grid. Add your goals in each category for year 3 first, then for year 2 and then identify your 1-year goals.

The 12 Categories	3 years	2 years	1 year
Health & Fitness			
Intellectual Life			
Emotional Life			
Character			
Spiritual Life			
Love Relationship			
Parenting			
Social Life			
Financial Life			
Career			
Quality of Life			
Life Vision			

Now, use part 2 of the grid (below), to break down your 1-year goals into monthly goals. Feel free to break these monthly goals down even further into weeks and even days. Repeat this for each of the 12 categories.

Month	Goal
January	
February	
March	
April	
May	
June	
July	
August	
September	
October	
November	
December	

CHAPTER 8

HOW TO ROCK YOUR OWN WORLD

> *"You owe yourself the love that you give so freely to other people."*
>
> -UNKNOWN

"I don't think you care about me."

I was traveling across Myanmar, with my wife on her birthday. I'd just finished singing the birthday song. I told her how much I loved her; how much I appreciated her support and the fact that she sees me and loves me for who I truly am.

But then I ruined it all with a thoughtless, mean comment.

"I don't think you care about me."

I was triggered because she had asked about the guest list for a party we were going to throw in L.A., the following month.

"I don't think you care about me."

Why would I say that? Why? She is among the most loving humans to have ever entered my life. She is amazing. She cares so much. What was up with me? What was happening?

If you and I get to meet one day, and I hope we do, you'll quickly realize that I'm an ambivert. I have extroverted tendencies, but the introvert in me usually rules the day. I find it hard to indulge in small talk. I need time to refuel. I gain energy doing things I want to do.

By myself.

But at that time in my life, when we were in Myanmar, alone time was just a fantasy. I was traveling all the time. My coaching schedule was packed. I was speaking on stages around the world. I was enrolling clients during those speaking gigs. On the outside, I was doing everything right but on the inside, I felt empty. Drained I had forgotten the one rule I had promised myself I would never forget...

Self-care. First. Before I rock the whole world, I have to rock my own world, first.

Until that point in my life, I had stayed true to that belief, and it had worked well for me. As a coach, you simply cannot serve others if your own tank is empty. If you are not at a place of peace, and bliss how can you share peace and bliss with others? How can you be present? How can you be sharp? Compassionate? Brave?

The realization hit me that day with my wife in Myanmar. I had put myself at the end of my own priority list. If I'm being totally honest, I wasn't even on my priority list.

It was time to get back on track and get to peak mental, spiritual and physical fitness. It was time to take care of the 4 states - the Mental State, the Brain State, the Body State, and the Spirit State.

The Mental State

What is the state of your mind? What makes it dip and go into a negative spiral? What are some of the key strategies you can use to make sure your mind stays at a peak, positive high?

Your mind influences everything. How you feel and how you learn.

How you act and react. Your mind is the source of all that you are. Your mind creates and holds your beliefs.

Negative mental chatter screws up your views and causes you to make decisions and take actions that are not in congruence with what's best for you. Negative mental chatter induces fear and paranoia. It is the reason we end up believing something that is not true. Something that we have created and accepted as "our story."

For the longest time, I suffered from negative mental chatter and over thinking. I still get into those cycles, where I can't stop thinking about something.

A few years ago, I had a situation with a girl :) You see I liked this girl, and she seemed to like me. But for some reason, every time we became close, she would end up pushing me away. It was clear we were attracted to each other, but it wasn't working out.

I eventually realized she had weird theories and beliefs about Indian men. About spiritual men. About successful men. Her past programming was blocking us from getting together.

But instead of accepting this about her, and moving on, I started spinning the situation in my head. I went from, "She doesn't love me!" to "No one loves me!" to "I'll never be happy again with a partner!" to "I'm no good. I'm just not enough!"

You've probably been on this ride. I call it the Downward Spiral Of Absolute Misery! It went on for some time before I finally became tired of feeling unhappy. I decided to coach myself out of it. I asked myself some powerful questions and committed to answering all of them honestly:

DOWNWARD SPIRAL OF MISERY

Is this the absolute truth? Or is it a figment of my imagination?

Does this mean anything in the long-term? In the big picture that is my life?

Will this moment define me, or will it educate me?

What can I learn from this situation?

What could be some scenarios that might be happening in the background?

Could all of this be about those scenarios and not about me?

What are the instances where cherished friends and loved ones have shown me love and gratitude?

What am I truly grateful for in my life?

These questions are simple, but they are powerful enough to change your Mind State from negative to positive. From down to upbeat. From chaos to clarity. If something's on your mind right now and you can't seem to escape the negative mental chatter, try answering these questions. They work.

Trust me.

The Brain State

The brain is different from the mind. When I refer to the brain, I'm talking about the chemical composition, neurons firing and all that fascinating, scientific stuff.

The reason why I separate the Mind State from the Brain State is that the mind is related to the emotional, erratic part of ourselves. The brain, on the other hand, is almost like a machine. You can get consistent, predictable results when you understand how your brain works and how to "program" it for high performance. We only use a fraction of the full capacity of our brain. We can activate more parts of the brain with vitamins, foods, and practices that support brain performance.

A common "drug" most of us turn to is caffeine, and it's a great hack to boost alertness and thinking capabilities - especially when you know exactly how to use it.

One of the best caffeine hacks on the planet is Bulletproof Coffee. I have been testing the Bulletproof concept for over 9 months at the time of writing, and the results have been phenomenal.

You can find out about the Bulletproof Diet and Bulletproof Coffee at bulletproof.com. Founder Dave Asprey attended A-Fest, where we interviewed him about the effects of food on our brain and other brain hacking strategies.

Watch Dave's talk here:
http://bit.ly/Biohacking-Dave

It's a profound discussion that may change the way you look at what you eat. Like me, you may be inspired to start thinking about food as fuel for your brain.

There are also other ways to enhance your brain performance - specifically the right and left brain. Studies have shown that most of us tend to operate from the left brain. This part of the brain is the source of logical decisions, process-oriented thinking, and rational judgments.

Your creativity, your ability to be in flow (as we discussed in Chapter 1), and your adaptability through the highs and lows of life and business, of being a better coach, arise from your right brain. One of the most powerful ways to optimize both the right and left brain is related to the 5 types of brain waves we experience.

Gamma

Gamma brain waves enhance right brain functionality. This frequency is activated during learning, memorizing, and processing information.

Delta

These are the slowest brain waves, and you experience this when you are in deep REM sleep. You experience less of this as you age.

Beta

The most active waveform and it's activated during your waking hours. Beta is in play during movement, hyperactivity, stress, and anxiety.

Alpha

You are in Alpha when you are calm and focused. This wave is activated during meditation and is the result of deep breathing and relaxation.

Theta

Unlocks creativity and plays a role in daydreaming, deep sleep and deepening your intuition.

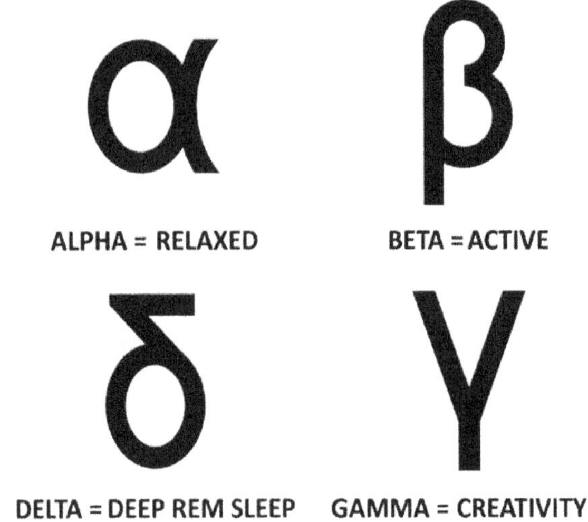

[Image source: Emotional GRIT: 8 Steps to Master Your Emotions, Transform Your Thoughts And Change Your World]

Meditation

Meditation is another effective and time-honored way to optimize your Brain State for focus, clarity, and enhanced performance. At Mindvalley, we've created an app dedicated to meditation with incredible teachers to help you develop those alpha brainwaves. The app is called Omvana.

You know more about Omvana here:
http://www.omvana.com/

While we were researching, what puts the brain on accelerated mode, we stumbled on a brain supplement company called, Neurohacker. Neurohacker produces a smart drug called "Qualia." Qualia is still in the early stages of development, but the results I've experienced are nothing short of amazing. Qualia not only increases focus but it also boost creativity. You tend to process things faster and get more done in less time.

You should also have a basic understanding of brain chemicals. Knowing how these chemicals work to elevate your state for the long-term and using this state to increase your creativity and connection with yourself and others, is one of the most transformative gifts you can give yourself.

Here are the 4 key brain chemicals you need to know about so you can manipulate them to boost your brain state.

Dopamine
Gets you to take action, become excited about new projects, relationships and life in general.

Serotonin
Low levels of this neurotransmitter triggers depression and anxiety. Serotonin has a direct correlation with your mood.

Endorphins
The happy hormone! Released during pain and stress (that's why you get that happy "high" after a great workout), and alleviates anxiety.

Oxytocin
The hug hormone. This is released with a 30 second hug, as well as when in the company of people you love and trust.

Note: My suggestions are based on my experience. Know that everyone's brain is different and this means what works for me may or may not work for you. Use these suggestions with discretion. Take what works and leave the rest. The choice is always yours.

The Body State

About 4 years ago I looked like a different person. I was about 10 kilograms (about 20 pounds) overweight with a body percentage of 47% which made me around 23 years older (I took an Inside Tracker test to discover this. I share more about this health service below). I had an ongoing (losing) battle with adult acne.

I looked sloppy. I survived my days with coffee and sugar hits. My body was in bad shape. As a result, the quality of my work suffered. On a good day, I was at 50% of my full potential. That was the highest level, I could reach.

As a coach, it's easy to get caught up with developing only your mind but neglecting to do the same for your body is a massive mistake. Your body is your vessel. If your body hurts, is in bad shape or if you lack energy and vitality, your emotions become chaotic.

You can't think clearly.

As I began to transform my body, first by incorporating walking into my daily routine, then via specific workouts, and finally dietary changes, I started to see what was previously hidden deep inside me. Possibilities opened up for me. I realized I could do more, and be more because of the support I had from my body.

As my body became healthier, my confidence went through the roof. There was more power in everything I did. I experienced a massive increase in my sense of self-worth. The transformation of my body led to the transformation of my entire life.

It was epic.

Don't feel like you have to implement a hundred different rules as you begin your journey to nurturing a healthier body. Go for the 80/20. One of the changes that will give you immediate results? Eliminate gluten and dairy from your diet. Yes, I know. This is a tough one. I suffered for the first 10 days but I stuck it out, and I began to see incredible positive changes in my body and in my energy. These changes motivated me to keep going.

I'm not a doctor, but here are a few health hacks I tried, after due research. I recommend you start your journey to a peak Body State with this list.

Give Up Gluten, Sugar, and Dairy

Growing up in India, I ate bread as a staple and sweets were the only way to end a meal. We drink milk when we wake up and go to sleep. It was hard for me to grasp That everything I had been doing my entire life, with food, was wrong. I was hesitant to change - just like you are right now as you read these words. Who wants to give up gluten, sugar, and dairy, right? But I tried it for a week, and I noticed an incredible boost in my energy. Test it out for yourself. Do it for 7 days. See what happens with your energy, alertness, and even your weight.

If you want to geek out on the research around gluten, go to this link: http://bit.ly/gluten-health

To kick your sugar habit, check out New York Times best-selling author, Dr. Mark Hyman's 10-day detox plan here:
http://bit.ly/10DayDetoxChallenge

Start Your Day with Supplements

Most foods no longer contain any nutritional value. Sad but true. The GMOs, and the way food is produced and cooked have destroyed all the natural goodness, which is why I recommend you start your day with a set of supplements. Before you start buying your supplements though, check out www.insidertracker.com.

InsideTracker is a service where you submit your blood sample at a nearby clinic. They run tests and send you an exact game plan that include the supplements you should take, and the exercises you should consider.

Having these results helps you discover the supplements that are perfect for you. At this time, this service is available only in the United States. If you live outside the U.S. please visit a nearby clinic, get your blood test done and ask your physician about your deficiencies and the supplements that can help you.

Try Intermittent Fasting

It doesn't work for everyone, but it worked like gangbusters for me! Intermittent fasting is when you eat only a few meals within a small window of time. Say, between 12pm and 6pm or 12pm to 8pm or 10am to 6pm.

The intermittent fasting movement is based on the premise that a daily routine of 3 full meals and snacks, turns our bodies into "sugar burning machines." This essentially means we burn the sugar in our bodies for energy. The problem with this is that we experience inconsistent energy levels all through the day. We experience energy crashes and start to crave a "pick me up." This is why we feel the need for coffee and sugary snacks. As a coach, you need to be at the top of your game. You need to maintain a steady state of energy to be at your best. Your body operates differently with intermittent fasting. It starts to burn fat for energy instead of sugar.

When we burn fat for energy 2 critical things happen:

(i) Fat burns in a more consistent way and your energy levels stay steady throughout the day.,
(ii) Because we start burning fat for energy we also lose unnecessary fat in our body.

Intermittent fasting can be hard to sustain. I mean really hard. Especially for the first 4 or 5 days. But like everything that's worth doing, it starts out hard but with time and persistence, it gets easy. Try it out and see if it works for you.

Include Good Fat in Your Diet

The fat-burning principle of intermittent fasting applies to your overall diet too. Start consuming more ghee, coconut oil, and grass-fed organic butter, which are great sources of good fat. You can cook with them; you can blend them in your coffee or tea. You also get good fats from avocados. Love those avocados!

If you want to test these ideas, talk to your physician first. Especially if you have pre-existing health conditions. Take your physician's advice if you are unsure. But remember that this is your body. Always make it a point to educate yourself, so you'll know what's right for you and what's not.

Go Crazy on Superfoods

Most of the food we consume is stripped of essential amino acids and minerals, so upleveling your nutrition with superfoods. Here are a few superfoods you can try:

Chaga is one of the most powerful antioxidants around. It grows in abundance on birch trees throughout Siberia. It is an adaptogen, and great for boosting your immunity.

Spirulina is one of the best sources of greens you can add to your meals. It gives your cells light and life, and it is one of the most nutrient-dense foods, on the planet.

The jury is out on whether turmeric is a superfood but I feel it deserves to be on this list. There are over 10,000 peer-reviewed articles on this humble yellow spice. It improves brain function, fights inflammation (especially if you fly a ton – so keep it in your travel health kit), and reduces joint pain like arthritis. It's also a mood enhancer, and helps to reverse insulin resistance.

Chia seeds are packed with fiber, zinc, calcium, and Omega-3. Chia boosts your metabolism and reduces sugar cravings. Dr. Axe goes into details here or go to this link https://draxe.com/chia-seeds-benefits-side-effects/

Sleep Smart

Having your smartphones and other tech tools near you, when you go to bed at night, is one of the worst mistakes you can make. The 'blue' light emitted by these devices stimulates your brain and will keep you awake. Sean Stevenson, best-selling author of Sleep Smarter, says you need to put away your phone and other work devices starting in the early evening hours. Think about incorporating night- time rituals to signal your brain and prep your body for sleep. You can try drawing a bath, light relaxing scented candles, do an evening meditation- anything calm and relaxing to help you unwind.

The Spirit State

Spirit. We all know it's there. None of us can truly explain it.

Here's my take: The spirit is energy that flows through your body. You can feel it sometimes when you enter a room. You can feel it sometimes when you are about to sign on a client, and it doesn't feel right.

Or when it feels fucking amazing.

You feel this "thing." This unseen energy and you need to protect it. It's a fickle thing. It gets excited with little things. It gets sad when someone says something mean or when an enrollment call doesn't go the way you want it to go.

I was first exposed to the spirit and the energy body when I was working with a colleague, and she talked about "reiki." This ancient practice from Japan shows you how to navigate your energy and help others too.

I was curious and I jumped right into it.

My conclusion? Reiki is transformational. So are several other spiritual modalities. It takes a certain level of belief to get yourself started on this type of energy work, but when you find that belief and go all in, it gives you the unique power to manage your energy like a ninja.

Note: The health hacks we share in this chapter are merely ideas - if you feel comfortable, and your doctor gives you the green light, go ahead and experiment with them. We tried these ideas on ourselves and they work incredibly well. Speak to your doctor before trying anything new on your body.

TOOLS

#1 Spirit and all that it entails is a complex topic. A good friend and author of the Duality program, Jeffrey Allen, talked about this complicated concept with beautiful simplicity on the A-Fest stage.

Watch Jeffery Allen explain Energy Secrets for Exceptional Communication and Connection: http://bit.ly/JeffreyAllen

#2 To reduce brain fog, and to see what else you can do to optimize brain performance, pick up a copy of Head Strong by Dave Asprey. Dave's work in this field is phenomenal and definitely worth checking out. https:// www.bulletproof.com/head-strong-book

#3 Click here to watch Vishen Lakhiani and Dave Asprey discuss brain-hacking or go to this link https:// http://bit.ly/Biohacking-Dave

#4 Find out more about intermittent fasting here: https://www.nerdfitness.com/blog/a-beginners-guide-to-intermittent-fasting/

#5 Find out more about Having a Stronger Brain here: https://blog.bulletproof.com/eat-fat-for-high-performance-brain/

#6 Find out more about the Bulletproof Diet here: https:// blog.bulletproof.com/wp-content uploads/2014/01/ Bulletproof-Diet-Infographic-Vector.pdf

#7 Click here to check out InsideTracker or go to this link https://www.insidetracker.com/

#8 Find out more about Dr. Mark Hyman here or follow this link www.drhyman.com

#9 Find out more about Dr. Mercola here or follow this link www.mercola.com

CHAPTER 9

HITTING THE PEAK

> *"You'll never change your life until you change something you do daily. The secret to your success is found in your daily routine."*
>
> -JOHN C. MAXWELL

In the previous chapter, I shared techniques you can use to get to a high- performance state where you are focused, present and productive. These techniques work, but most of them take a while to kick in. So, what do you do if you need to hit the peak, fast?

That's what this chapter is about.

You'll discover how to switch to a peak emotional state, in an instant. I'm focusing on your emotional state and not any of the other 3 states – body, spirit or brain – because the emotional state is the most volatile and the most difficult to control.

It is also the state that will make the biggest difference on your overall performance, when you learn to shift it, in the moment.

The tools in the following pages will help you combat the daily stressors of life in minutes so you can rise above and perform at the highest level as a coach no matter what else is going on around you.

Morning Bliss

Can you tell me how you currently create a little bit of "Morning Bliss" for yourself, each day? If you're going, "Morning Bliss, Ajit? What on earth are you talking about?" I can already guess what your mornings look like right now!

You wake up and probably hit the snooze button more than once. When you finally manage to drag yourself out of bed, you realize it's later than you thought. You end up getting dressed in a rush. You down a quick cup of coffee before diving into your work day. If you have a few minutes to spare, you grab an on-the-go snack for breakfast – probably something unhealthy, and straight out of a box or package.

As you sit down in front of your computer, you feel distracted and maybe even a little annoyed. You struggle with poor concentration and lack of clarity all day. A Morning Bliss practice or ritual will help you overcome all of this so you can start your day from a place of inner peace and power.

Master Your Day

Personal practices and rituals are used by some of the most successful people in the world, to create an inner environment of strength and stamina. Studies have shown that certain morning routines and habits have can set you up for a successful, productive day.

I want you to think of your Morning Bliss routine as your sacred, personal time. It's a powerful and effective way to prime your mind, body, and soul so you can master your day. You've probably had your clients do this, but it's very easy to forget to do it for yourself. I know, I have!

My co-author Neeta shared a special combination of Morning Bliss activities during a talk she gave to a global group of engineers at the Google headquarters in Mountain View, California. She uses a handy acronym – 4MAS – to remember these activities easily. Neeta believes and I agree – that a Morning Bliss routine is a must if you want to manage your daily stress levels, effectively. It should be a part of what Neeta calls, your Emotional GRIT kit.

The 4MAS Method

4MAS can be chunked down into 4 components – Music, Meditation, Movement, and Mantra followed by Acknowledgment and Sensation:

Music

Music is a powerful mood-shifter. The music you listen to and the lyrics you hear can instantly influence your emotional state. If you listen to an upbeat song first thing in the morning, you'll induce positive thoughts. If you listen to a song with unhappy or angry lyrics, you'll soon find yourself feeling miserable or annoyed. This mood is likely to filter into the rest of your day. So, pick your morning music with care.

Here are a few playlists that I regularly turn to when I want to motivate and inspire myself and others. These lists are regularly updated on Spotify.

- Dance Party. Want to get into the groove and move? Here's a dance playlist I use as part of my Morning Bliss routine. http://bit.ly/dance-party-spotify
- Electronic Chill. Great as background music when you are working in a café. http://bit.ly/electronic-chill-spotify
- Deep Focus. Allows focused concentration for prolonged periods. Perfect for writing, thinking and reading. http://bit.ly/deep-focus-spotify

Meditation and Mindfulness

You've probably heard of at least a few of the countless benefits of mindfulness and meditation. If you're still unsure or you'd like to know more go here:
http://bit.ly/Mindfulness-Benefits

I like to start my morning with 10 to 25 minutes of traditional, sitting meditation. I usually include creative visualization and gratitude exercises as part of my practice. Here are some guided meditations and tracks that I turn to again and again:

- Devi Prayer. Listen to it here: http://bit.ly/DeviPrayer
- Meditation music for your personal mantras. Listen to it here: http://bit.ly/Mantras-Meditation

Other than traditional meditation, another effective way to get into a meditative, mindful state is to control your breath. I was recently introduced to Holotropic Breathwork, and I cannot recommend it enough. This method of breathing allows you to experience deep healing and altered states of mind. It can help you recharge your energy, and it's one of the most effective methods to get back into a peak emotional state in just a few minutes.

You can know more here:
http://bit.ly/Ultraculture-Breathwork

Movement

Just a little bit of physical movement in the morning will shift your energy and help you conquer your day. If you enjoy formal workouts or training (by the way, good for you if you do!) start your day with a favorite workout. If not, include at least some sort of activity that gets your body moving and positive energy flowing. Think about this: have you ever seen someone dance and be pissed off at the same time?

TOOLS

Here are some ideas to get your body moving:

Dance to 3 songs

Do 3 sets of 10 push ups

Swim for 10 minutes

Do 2 sets of 21 squats

Do weight exercises for 8 minutes

Keep in mind that any movement is better than no movement at all.

Mantra

Traditionally a mantra is a set of positive or spiritual words or sentences that you chant over and over again.

Here's my definition: a mantra is a set of positive words such as a quote, thought, statement or text that leaves me feeling inspired and motivated. No chanting or repetition required! To me, a mantra can even be an upbeat podcast or audiobook on personal growth. I've found mantras have the power to boost my emotional state almost immediately.

My morning mantra is usually a personal development book I'm reading or a positive podcast that I enjoy. Here are some of the podcasts I listen to regularly:

Modal Health Show:
http://theshawnstevensonmodel.com/podcasts/
This is Your Life:
https://michaelhyatt.com/thisisyourlife
Entrepreneur On Fire:
https://www.eofire.com/itunes

Acknowledgement

This part of your Morning Bliss routine is about expressing gratitude and appreciation to those who have supported you and who continue to support you in your journey to success and happiness.

This includes YOU.

Always acknowledge yourself, your loved ones, your partners, your team members for all that they do and the joy they bring to your life.

I also share 3 wins with my partner, every night. It gets me to see my day with fresh eyes – I realize just how much I've accomplished. Our minds are wired to hone in on what's wrong not what's right. Celebrating 3 wins at the end of your day forces you to identify the good that happens in your life and in your business, on a daily basis.

In his great book, *The Happiness Advantage,* leading expert on happiness, Shawn Achor talks about a gratitude experiment that he conducted when he was hired as a consultant for a large company.

The idea was for a team member to send a note of gratitude to a different team member, first thing in the morning, every single day for a month. At first, people were incredibly resistant to the idea. This was a high-level corporate environment. Gratitude notes weren't exactly the norm but, they decided to go ahead and give it a try, anyway.

After a month Achor ran tests and found that the team that participated in the experiment was a lot happier, more productive and had achieved amazing goals. This happened in *just one month.*

Expressing your appreciation to someone in your life can do the same for you – and for those who receive your gratitude.

Sensation

Your job as a coach allows you to grow and expand in amazing ways but running your own coaching practice can also be a limiting experience. Think about it - you are usually either serving clients or working on your business. Consciously introducing varied sensations into your life can mix things up, increase happiness, and improve productivity.

Here are some ways to tap into and explore the world with all your senses:

Scents

Keep various bottles of essential oils handy. Drop these oils into a diffuser or just open the bottle cap and breathe in the scent whenever you need to center yourself. You can also burn scented candles or incense.

Human interaction

Not in a client/coach way but pure human interaction… *just because.* Create opportunities to play and have fun with your partner, friends, and loved ones. Touch. Hug. Hold. Get a massage. Go to a coffee shop and talk to strangers. Be open to random conversations and find ways to physically connect.

Laugh

Be warned: this one can lead you down a rabbit hole because once you start, it's hard to stop! On the days when work feels like a punishment, or anytime you need to boost your energy and mood, go to good ol' YouTube and watch funny moments captured on camera. My favorite videos include standup comic clips by Kevin Hart, Jimmy Kimmel, Sarah Silverman, Ellen DeGeneres and of course, Louis CK. Whatever floats your boat. Get some laughs in.

Image from Emotional GRIT: 8 steps to manage your emotions, transform your thoughts, & change your world

Ask Yourself

How will I incorporate these ideas and concepts into my mornings? How can I create a Morning Bliss routine that sets me up for peak performance throughout the day? Which concepts will I use regularly?

CHAPTER 10

EMOTIONALLY FIT

> *"When life sucks you under, you can kick against the bottom, break the surface, and breathe again. You choose. It is the hard days — the times that challenge you to your very core — that will determine who you are. You will be defined not just by what you achieve, but by how you survive."*
>
> -SHERYL SANDBERG

Emotional fitness covers a range of factors such as emotional resilience, character traits, stability, inner strength, and a high Emotional Quotient or EQ.

Neeta surveyed over 500 entrepreneurs, startup founders, corporate executives, leaders, moms, and business titans from all over the world.

The verdict was the same.

If you're looking to rock the journey to emotional fitness so you can enhance your business, make a difference for your clients, and stand out as an extraordinary coach, the following 11 characteristics are your essential ingredients:

Authenticity

Your willingness to show up as *yourself* without worrying about what other people may think of you.

Drive

Your ability to stay motivated and keep on going no matter what.

Enthusiasm

What is the attitude that you bring to your live and written or recorded interactions? What is the energy behind your emails, your networking events and workshops? Your vibe shifts everything. Enthusiasm is contagious and can even transform the outcome of your enrollment conversations with potential clients.

Courage

Your willingness to share your voice, your opinion, and how you serve your clients, unapologetically. It includes the risks you are willing to take in your business.

Curiosity

This is a deep understanding and need to know more. It's about wanting to understand why, to pursue the unknown, gain a different perspective or a different thought process, with a sense of openness and expansion.

Presence

Presence is the foundation for Intentional work. Your efficiency and productivity, skyrocket when you choose your thoughts wisely, without mental clutter.

Empathy

Extremely important in your work as coach. This is about being aware and open to the feelings of others and about understanding the perception and the perspective of the other person. This is the art of finding the reasons behind the decisions, and thought processes of others.

Self-Compassion

The understanding that you are doing the best that you can. Removing the pressures and heavy expectations that you have on yourself to 'get it all done'.

Adaptability

Being flexible when challenges, unwanted, and unexplainable situations arise to test your internal strength. Adaptability also includes having a certain level of detachment to your clients' outcomes, and in your business. It allows you to flow with ease and achieve greater success.

Vulnerability

Celebrate the things that makes you human – including the imperfections and the mistakes. Being vulnerable builds trust, and highlights your unique personality, gifts and talents.

Resilience

Related to how you handle the curveballs of life and business - the 'in the red' income months, or a sudden, overwhelming influx of new clients. This is about effectively failing forward, and honoring the experience and lessons as you keep moving forward.

These characteristics create grit - you rising again after getting your 15th rejection.

You carrying on with the presentation after you launch your online program and no one buys.

You being able to repeatedly present your Facebook lives, meetups, and workshops even if there's only 1 or 2 or zero people watching.

You committing to being consistent and trying again and again, every step of the way.

This is what emotional fitness is made of.

It's the difference between you and those who give up.

It's the thing that will hold you strong as you support future clients who keep saying NO to the life you wish to help them build because they are just too afraid.

Build your "emotional fitness muscles" to be stronger *for them.*

To see what they cannot see.
To help the make their dreams a reality.

Ask yourself

- Which of the 11 characteristics do you already embody?
- Which of them do you wish to strengthen, as a coach?
- Which of the 11 characteristics (select 3 max) would be absolute game-changers in your business, if you made them a central part of your personality?

The answers to these questions will give you an amazing place to begin building your emotional fitness muscles. So let's start working out!

CHAPTER 11

TOOLS TO BUILD AN UNBREAKABLE CENTERPIECE

> *"On the mountains of truth you can never climb in vain. Either you will reach a point higher up today, or you will be training your powers so that you will be able to climb higher tomorrow."*
>
> -Friedrich Nietzsche

I want you to be a strong centerpiece. To be powerful. Extraordinary. And I want you to know it's possible.

I also want you to know it isn't easy.

For "extraordinary" to happen, you need to get into a peak state and stay in a peak state.

I've already shared a list of methods, techniques, ideas, and tools you can use to become a high-performer in your life and work.

The following are the best of the best – the top tools - you can use to change your state. Some of these tools are free; some are paid. In my opinion, free or paid, every one of these is worth your time and money.

The Evercoach Summit Playlist

This is a highly energizing, upbeat Spotify playlist we developed especially for the Evercoach Summit. It's regularly updated, so you'll always find new, fresh songs added to the list. You can find it here: http://bit.ly/EC-Summit

6-Phase Meditation

This meditation can be used at any time. It will help you step into a peak state in mere minutes. Go to http://bit.ly/6Phase

The Achiever's Method

The Achiever's Method is my baby :) I developed this method for me, and when people who know me started asking me about it, I decided to share it with the world. You can find out more about the Achiever's Method here: www.ajitnawalkha.com/achiever

Your methodology

RESULTS FIRST

CHAPTER 12

RESULTS FIRST

"You don't concentrate on risks. You concentrate on results. No risk is too great to prevent the necessary job from getting done."

-CHUCK YEAGER

I was at a mastermind group meeting with 6 and 7-figure business owners. There was so much ego in the room you could almost reach out and touch it. Everyone was ready to talk about how much money they made, how many goals they'd achieved, and how successful they were.

I was the new kid. I didn't have a big ego. I didn't even know what I was doing. I knew I was successful but I guess it hadn't gone to my head. As I moved around the room, getting to know people, I found a group that seemed to have a cooler vibe. They were less pretentious. I connected with one individual in particular.

Let's call him Sol.

Sol ran a thriving coaching business. He was a successful coaches' coach and his business was expanding at a tremendous rate. He was happy about that but he was starting to feel immense pressure. He had no idea how he was going to sustain that level of growth and he knew he needed help.

But here's the million-dollar question: Who does a coach's coach go to for business coaching?

When you're a coach who's already achieved a massive level of success, it's hard to find another coach you can turn to for solid insight and advice. You already have strong ideas about the world. You believe you know what to believe and what not to believe.

Sol was willing to be coached, but he was also resisting it. He was worried he wouldn't get what he needed to grow his business. We were having dinner with the group when Sol first told me he needed a coach. He also confided about his resistance. We fell into a deep discussion and after dinner, we stepped out for a walk.

I kept digging to get to the root of his resistance. We both kept digging.

Eventually, Sol began to see the light. He started to feel motivated. Inspired. He was eager to continue the conversation but I was flying out the next day. There was a small window of time when we could meet; it would have to be in the early morning before I left for the airport.

Sol was more than happy to wake up early and connect with me over breakfast. This time, the questions went deeper. Much deeper. Before we'd even finished the conversation, Sol was ready for more and he told me so. It would be the first time I'd offered someone a "formal" coaching package. I took a deep breath and made my offer.

$15,000 for an entire year.

I could barely get the words out of my mouth before Sol said yes. It was so easy. I could hardly believe it.

The Real Challenge

There's an insidious belief in the coaching industry – enrolling clients is THE biggest challenge you'll face as a coach. But that's not true. The real challenge is to serve powerfully. To serve in a way where your clients experience lasting transformation.

That's what coaching is about. It's an experience. Not a product.

Just think how ridiculous it sounds when someone hears a description of what you do as a coach: "*My job is to sit with you and talk*. Oh, and you need to pay me to do that."

This would make no sense to a person who has never experienced coaching but when you've had sessions with an outstanding coach, you know just how life-changing a simple "talk" can be.

As a coach, you have to have your clients and potential clients experience you. Your coaching. Your work.

You need to be able to move into that energy and feel what they feel. They need to be able to see why talking to you will be a transformational experience for them.

When I met Sol, I didn't have any training on how to make one-on-one sales. I hadn't put together a coaching package. I didn't even know what I would do with Sol during our year together. But I did know how to ignite the spark of greatness inside him. I knew how to get him to see a whole new set of possibilities that would give him great results in his life and business.

Most people go through life without anyone cheering them on and encouraging them to grow and change. To aspire for more. To achieve. That's what you need to do as a coach. That's your real job.

You're the one who holds space for others. You're the one who believes in them. You're the one who supports them. Inspires them. Motivates them to keep going even when they think they can't.

But before you get to do all of that, your first duty is to earn their trust. The most powerful way to do that?

Deliver results. Help them solve their problems. Help them create a clear map to get to where they want to go. Paint a picture of what the outcome will look like. Get them results, first.

Go Deep

Coaching involves a mix of knowledge and technique. Knowledge is important and technique is crucial. These are the tools that will get you started as a coach. You need to be knowledgeable about human psychology, and human behaviour. You need to have great skills and techniques around asking the right questions.

So, keep increasing your knowledge.

Keep practicing your techniques. Keep coaching until it's as natural as breathing.

But remember this: coaching from a place of pure knowledge and technique will only get you so far. When you want to go from average to extraordinary, you need to step into a whole other level.

A level called *insight-based coaching*.

If you continue to grow and develop your skills as a coach, it won't be long before you start working with high-performers. These are clients who are far more successful that you are in all areas of life. These are world class leaders, CEOs, experts and specialists.

When you get to this stage, when you're coaching high-performers, it gets harder and harder to prepare ahead of time for what may show up. Techniques will fail you at this stage. Theory and knowledge will fail you too. When you're playing at that level, there is only one thing that can help you coach: showing up with present moment awareness.

Present moment awareness is *everything*. Awareness around what your client is saying. What she's not saying.

What she's doing.
The sound of her voice. Her body language.

When you are absolutely present and aware, you are tuned into an untapped reservoir of intelligence that you can access purely through intuition. This reservoir will reveal the questions you need to ask. The conversation you need to have. The kind of energy and environment you need to create for each, individual client.

So, get into the present moment. Show up fully. No holding back. Give them the coaching experience they need.
Get them results, first.

Ask Yourself?

What are the experiences, programs, retreats, excursions, and masterminds you've been drawn to recently? Commit to attending at least one or two transformational live events each year. Other than live events, what other ways can you challenge yourself to add more depth to your personal growth, be exposed to new ways of thinking, and help yourself open up to new perspectives? How can you shake up your current views so you can create even more powerful, and effective results for your clients?

CHAPTER 13

THE INTELLIGENCE WITHIN

"Follow your instincts. That's where true wisdom manifests itself."

-OPRAH WINFREY

I love the structure that comes with systems and strategies. Structure in my coaching gives me confidence when I'm working with a client. In my mind, structure equals power.

But structure can also hold you back, as a coach.

I've been coaching other coaches for a while now, and I thought I'd nailed what works and what doesn't until I met best-selling author and legendary transformational and leadership coach, Michael Neill.

Michael has written 6 books including, *Supercoach: 10 Secrets to Transform Anyone's Life*. At the time of this writing, his 7th book is about to greet the world. Since he's been doing it for a long time and he's a world class coach, you'd think Michael would be all about systems and strategies. At least that's what I thought.

Turns out, I was wrong.

A Vessel for Wisdom

Sitting at a café on a sunny day in Santa Monica sipping our Bulletproof Coffee (see Chapter 8 for more on Bulletproof Coffee), Michael and I had a heart to heart about the world of coaching. We talked about everything - structures, challenges, and potential solutions.

At one point, Michael turned to me and said, "I've met many people in the industry, Ajit. A lot of them are assholes. You are definitely not an asshole."

I was honored. And relieved.

Then Michael shared something deeply profound. He started talking about "innate intelligence."

He described this concept as, "An extraordinary intelligence that exists beyond our personal intellect."

You might have experienced this in your work as a coach. Usually, it goes something like this: you're in a coaching session. You're there for your client. Fully present. Suddenly, you say something that blows their mind and creates an instant, positive transformation in them. After the session, you think, "Where the heck did that come from? That was good!"

That was innate intelligence at work.

Unfortunately, most coaches don't consciously tap into it. We rely on our thinking mind - our intellect - to find answers to problems and challenges. But innate intelligence is far more powerful than the thinking mind. It's a far more effective way to find ideal solutions for your clients.

Innate intelligence flows naturally. This is not a step-by-step, systematic, structured approach to results-driven coaching. It's based entirely on instant insights that you intuitively receive during a coaching session or conversation. The only way to open the door to innate intelligence is to listen closely – intently and with deep present moment awareness – to your client. You need to be authentic, present and aware.

When you do that, you become a channel - a vessel for wisdom - to come through for your clients. I'll be honest. I found it hard to grasp this concept at first. I wasn't sure if Michael was a crazy mofo or an undisputable genius. I discovered the answer when I tried his method.

He's an undisputable genius.

Show Up And Rain

When you tap into innate intelligence, your ability to coach effectively, and authentically will skyrocket. You'll show up and rain.

The following excerpt from one of Michael's powerful coaching videos captures what it means to show up and rain:

"...I was listening to an old recording of Anthony de Mello, the enlightened Jesuit, and he was in a dialogue with, I assume a student... I don't know.

They were talking about helping.

He said, "I've given up, I used to try to help, but it never worked out very well. So, I don't help anymore."

And the student said, "Well what do you do instead?" and Anthony said, "I rain." It wasn't I "reign." It was I RAIN.

His student asked what he meant, and he said, "Well, I show up, and I do what I do. I am who I am. Some people like the rain and some people don't."

If the rain falls on fertile soil things grow and if the rain falls on dry soil it makes the soil fertile for future growth.

If the rain falls on a rock, nothing happens. That's really what we've got. Show up and rain."

Go beyond structures. Be present. Listen with your entire being. Share from the heart.

Become a vessel for wisdom. A channel for innate intelligence. Show up and rain.

Ask Yourself

"How can I be more present when I'm coaching? How can I connect with my intuition? How can I tap into innate intelligence?"

TOOLS

#1 Watch Michael's powerful video
Coach Like The Rain
http://bit.ly/CoachLikeRain

#2 You can experience Michael's genius through his books, seminars, and coaching intensives. Visit Michael's website here or go to this link
https://www.michaelneill.org/

CHAPTER 14

UNDERSTANDING YOUR CLIENT

> *"The noblest pleasure is the joy of understanding."*
>
> -Leonardo Da Vinci

The world's greatest coaches work hard to understand their clients because they know it is the only way to ignite rapid, permanent transformations. They use various methodologies to gain insights and knowledge on what makes their clients tick.

They look for answers to questions like:

What are the real reasons behind a client's decisions?
Who and what do their clients value and cherish?
What are they looking for in their lives and in their work?
How do they view themselves and the world?

This understanding allows these coaches to create amazing - sometimes even miraculous - results for their clients.

Results that establish their expertise as a world class coach.

Results that create a long wait list of clients who can't wait to work with them.

These smart coaches know that understanding their clients is the secret sauce to becoming an extraordinary coach.

In this chapter, I'll show you how to dive deep into your client's psyche and internal emotional landscape. I'll also share the powerful methodology I use to evaluate a client at the start of our time together.

The Paradigm of Desires

One of the most powerful and effective ways to get to know your client deeply is to understand their decision-making process.

If you've taken a Psychology 101 class, you've probably heard of Abraham Maslow. He's the guy who gave us the following chart which captures 6 basic human needs. These are the needs that influence pretty much every decision we ever make in our lives.

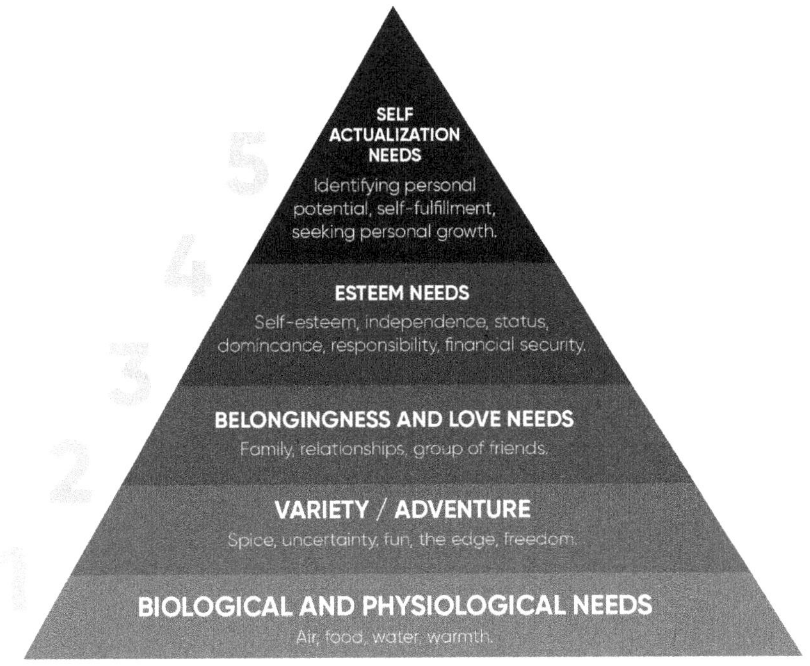

I've used Maslow's Hierarchy of Needs, also popularly known as Maslow's Pyramid, as a jumping off point to create the Paradigm of Desires. Coaches can use this to shed light on their client's decision- making process.

It's a model that consists of 6 categories that will help you understand your client's deepest desires - the desires that inspire and motivate them in all areas of their lives.

Safety and Security

These are basic, biological needs. Food, shelter – everything your client needs to feel safe, and (financially) secure. This can show up as a desire to have a job with a monthly income, and a 401k plan, a desire to meet and settle down with a life partner, a desire to create consistent revenue in a business and many others.

Variety

This is about the desire to enjoy the element of surprise and spontaneity in life. Clients who value variety are motivated by a deep desire for freedom. They thirst for excitement and fun. This desire can show up as a love for travel, adrenaline-pumping sports, new projects, or a variety of partners and romantic relationships.

Connection

This one is about community. It can show up as a client's desire for solid family relationships, and lifelong friends. She may feel incomplete unless she is connected to an organization or belief system such as a religious group, spiritual system or even a Yoga community.

Significance

Clients who seek significance want to be seen as unique. They want to stand out from the crowd. Ego can play a massive role here. The desire for significance can show up as a strong urge to climb the corporate ladder or collect achievements, accolades, and material possessions.

Growth

Growth is about learning, growing, and stimulating the intellect. Clients who desire growth tend to operate from a place of curiosity. They are into knowledge accumulation and evolving as a human being. In business, this desire shows up as a constant need for improvement, innovation and enhancement of work performance, and business techniques and strategies.

Contribution

Does your client dream of having a positive impact on the world, paying it forward, or changing lives? This usually shows up as a desire to give money, time or skills to their community, doing acts of philanthropy or choosing work that allows them to serve. Many coaches fall into this category because serving others is their #1 desire.

Now that you've been introduced to the Paradigm of Desires, you can easily identify what motivates your client and her current mindset.

Beyond The Paradigm

Beyond the Paradigm of Desires, there are 5 other major needs that you must take into account when you want to understand your clients. While the Paradigm of Desires influences decisions, the following needs tend to influence your client's thoughts, feelings, and actions.

#1 Love

The most common, universal element of all. The need for love is part of our makeup as humans. It is a built-in driver of our actions.

#2 Belonging

From the moment we are born, we are motivated by the need to belong and to be a part of a group or community. We want to be included by others. To be accepted by society.

#3 Worthiness

We all want to feel worthy. This powerful need is the reason why rejection of any kind hurts so much. Feeling worthy is also connected to confidence and self-belief.

#4 Enough-ness

Just about everyone struggles with this one – feeling like we're not enough. This causes us to overcompensate. We turn into people pleasers and perfectionists. Clients who need enough-ness will constantly push themselves to do more, be more and achieve more.

#5 Validation

This is about feeling appreciated and acknowledged for our efforts and accomplishments. We want to be recognized, seen, heard, and desired, by others. It's in our nature as human beings.

Understanding your clients' needs and desires will give you a massive head start in creating results that will inspire them to push past imagined limitations and get to a space where they're operating at their highest level. You'll gain an understanding about their life story, the way they see themselves and you'll have accurate insights on their perspective of the world.

While you're at it, it's also good to get clear on your personal needs and desires. This will help you understand your behaviors, actions, and beliefs so you can create value-driven goals and focus in your life and business.

Use the Paradigm of Desires along with the 5 additional human needs as the fabric, foundation, and framework to assess your clients, understand their actions and behaviors and gain an insider's look into their decision- making process.

Evaluating Emotional Intelligence

Harvard Associate Professor and best-selling author Daniel Goldman coined the term emotional intelligence which reflects an individual's potential to master self-awareness, self-management, social awareness, and relationship management.

Emotional intelligence is now widely accepted as one of the key indicators of success in business, leadership, and life.

As a coach, you must learn to quickly and accurately identify and understand your client's level of emotional intelligence. You must learn how to detect and work with their emotions in the moment, and in the long-term, so you can lead them out of chaos and into stability. This will help them operate with a sense of self-belief and confidence that allows them to hit or even surpass their goals.

Emotional intelligence begins with a baseline understanding of the spectrum of human emotions. It involves developing an awareness of your client's emotional state and emotional health. To help you with this, here are some of the most common positive and negative emotional states we experience on a daily basis.

POSITIVE EMOTIONAL STATES

compassionate / creative / connected / successful / appreciated / deserving / loving / playful / calm / excited / thoughtful / happy joyous / kind / content / motivated / peaceful / supported / valued inspired / purposeful / enthusiastic / invigorated / friendly / driven empowered / confident / attractive / abundant / limitless / present fulfilled / relaxed

NEGATIVE EMOTIONAL STATES

anxious / sad / empty / alone / numb / insecure / unconfident self-critical / misunderstood / incompetent / isolated / unsupported outcast / hopeless / unloved / worrisome / unattractive / stressed resentful / depressed / jaded / bored / inadequate / inferior frustrated / confused / angry / overwhelmed / unhappy / outdated envious / judged

Image from Emotional GRIT: 8 steps to master your emotions, transform your thoughts, and change your world.

Your clients are likely to struggle with painful emotions in the negative spectrum such as anxiety, stress, sadness, insecurity, worry, and fear which is why they need your help and support.

Some of the most of the common drugs prescribed in the U.S. are antidepressants and medication designed to improve cognitive function and elevate emotional states. This shows there are countless people who are experiencing powerful negative emotions that hold them back from living life to the fullest. Many of them are desperately turning to drugs as a way out.

It is your duty as a coach to learn how to use your skills to guide the people who come to you for help - your clients - so they can appropriately handle their emotions and have the ability to bring themselves back to a place of emotional stability and strength. This is a vital tool to add to your repertoire of methodologies as a coach.

Is Your Client Ready?

Other than learning about your client's motivations behind their decisions, their actions, beliefs, thoughts and emotional strength, it is also very important to evaluate your client's readiness. Before you begin your journey with a client, you must make sure they are ready for the transformations they say they are looking for.

Below is one of the key coaching methodologies I use when I'm evaluating if a client is ready to go to the next level and beyond:

1. Assess their awareness, or ability to 'GROW'.
2. The ability to 'REVEAL' or accept the situation they are in.
3. Only then will they be ready to 'COMMIT' to change or 'INNOVATE'.
4. And then proceed with 'ACTION' & 'TRANSFORMATION. This is the GRIT process, and it was created by my co-author Neeta.

GRIT is the acronym for Grow, Reveal, Innovate, and Transform. These 4 principles, will allow you to assess your client's level of willingness, awareness, and openness which are vital for rapid transformation.

Here is a closer look at **GRIT**:

Grow (Awareness)

- Self-mastery, Self-Belief, Self-Discovery
- Understanding stories, limiting beliefs
- Demystifying habits and patterns of behavior
- Finding internal purpose and mission

Reveal (Acceptance, Acknowledge, Celebrate)

- Stepping out of fear
- Creating a new story
- Diving into beliefs and values
- Celebrating strengths and understanding shortcomings
- Forgiving the past, letting go, and creating healthy boundaries

Innovate (Commit, Challenge, Change, Redefine)

- Challenging the current perspective
- Understanding the ego
- Gaining new perspective

Transform (Action, Strategy, Next Steps)

- Understanding purpose
- Elevating potential
- Building new anchor points and foundations
- Staying accountable

If your client is ready, you can then take them through the GRIT process to give them powerful results. The extra benefit is that you get to refine your coaching abilities at the same time.

The Honeymoon Stage

Understanding your new client is like the "honeymoon stage" in a new relationship.

Here's what I mean...

Imagine this: you finally have the chance to date that person. The one who lights up every room they step into. Everyone who meets them is absolutely mesmerized, and you are no exception ;-).

In the early days – "the honeymoon stage" - you do whatever it takes to connect with the other person because you are fascinated and captivated by everything they say and do.

So, you listen with your whole being. You pay attention to every detail. You try your best to understand who they are, how they feel, and what they think. You make sure they feel safe, as you get to know them. You even share some of your most intimate secrets, and this intensifies the emotional bond between the two of you.

This is how you should approach your new clients, your current clients and your future clients. If you want to be an extraordinary coach, stay in the "honeymoon stage" with your clients.

Give your clients your full attention, your full awareness and seek to know who they truly are by getting to know their needs and desires – even the ones that they may not openly share with you. Build trust.

Serving your clients and guiding them toward amazing results and rapid transformations in their life and business can only come from deep understanding and trust. It is the most sacred shared experience you can provide as a coach.

TOOLS

#1 Think of 2 clients, past or present, (or potential clients).

Based on the Paradigm of Desires, what are their top 2 desires? Based on the 5 additional needs, what are their top 2 needs? How can you help them using "GRIT"?

How can you help them Grow, Reveal, Innovate, and Transform? What is the real story behind their pain? The reason they came to you? How have you, transformed them (describe a situation, scenario)? What was the desired outcome? Was it achieved? What seems to be the block or limiting factor that could be holding them back from the desired result?

#2 Knowing and understanding what you know now, describe 3 ways you can use GRIT to discover your clients' needs and desires so you can serve them powerfully.

#3 Dive deeper into the powerful GRIT process with Neeta's book, Emotional GRIT: 8 Steps to Master Your Emotions, Transform Your Thoughts and Change Your World. Get the book here https://emotionalgrit.com/

CHAPTER 15

ASK POWERFUL QUESTIONS

> *"The greatest gift is not being afraid to question."*
>
> -RUBY DEE

Powerful questions. This is THE coaching element that separates a so-so coach from one who is extraordinary.

Powerful questions guide clients to discover who they are and what they want. Powerful questions allow clients to find solutions that are right for them. To accept those solutions. To embody those solutions.

Powerful questions inspire incredible personal transformations. They ignite revolutionary changes. The good news is you don't have to learn how to ask powerful questions through trial and error. It's not a hit or miss game. There are specific methods you can use to become truly great at this skill.

Listen with Your Entire Being

The most important component of asking powerful questions is knowing how to listen.

You must create space for your client by listening with your entire being. Do this when your client is talking about their challenge. Do it when they are thinking out loud as they seek answers to their problems.

Listen well, and you'll even hear their internal dialogue, which will be reflected in what they say to you. Be mindful that you are not arriving at your own conclusions and incorporating your personal insights into the mix, based on your truth.

Blaine Bartlett, the author of Three Dimensional Coaching, talks about how humans communicate not just through language, but with the mind, emotions and the physical body. When you are listening to your clients are you listening to what they're communicating through their emotions, their mind, and their body? Or are you focusing only on their words?

Listening intently, deeply and with presence is the key to creating extraordinary results for your clients. Always listen to explore and to understand. Not to react or respond.

Your aim is to take your clients on a journey to truly feeling what they feel and finding out *why* they feel that way. Your role is to help them dive deep into their emotions and discover where those emotions come from and what they mean. This will allow your clients to get to know themselves - their desires, fears, motivations, and beliefs – in a way that they've never known before.

Here are a few powerful questions I regularly turn to during sessions with clients:

- What does this mean to you?
- Imagine if you get to that stage that you're aiming for, what would that look like?
- What do you need to know to get to this outcome?
- What are some possible options you can try? What other ways can you explore to achieve that?

Be Outrageous

The transformational energy of asking powerful questions is perfectly captured by Steve Chandler in his book, the Prosperous Coach which he co-authored with my good friend Rich Litvin.

Here's what Steve says:

"One of the coaches in a prior school I ran had an $18,000 month. She used to have months that were closer to $3,000, but one way she boosted her income was by ruling out lunch, dinner and coffee as options for that first meeting with a coaching prospect.

Those options are from 1950s' sales books that say you should first get to know someone socially.

But the truth is that it actually diminishes the chances you'll land a coaching client if you have lunch with them first and establish your relationship as a social one.

What do you do instead? Throw them in the slammer.

Get a small room in a tin warehouse by the waterfront with a single lightbulb hanging from a frayed wire in the ceiling and one small table and two metal chairs and go full Mossad on them. Or whatever your version of that would be. But you must create a clearing in which transformation has a chance to happen.

If you just "have lunch" they will never feel the value of coaching. They'll just think you are an amiable, affable, social person who is fun to chat with—but why pay big bucks for that?"

Okay, so going full Mossad on your clients may feel like a bit much, but you get the idea. Asking questions no one else dares to ask will shift your clients' energy. It will get them thinking.

It will get them to move. To take action.

Change.
Grow.

So, when you're asking powerful questions, go ahead and be outrageous. Be brave. Be bold because you are doing something very important and valuable for your clients...

You are giving them permission to explore that which is hidden within them. Those beliefs and ideas they hold on to but which do not serve them. The thoughts that feel scary to explore. That dreams and aspirations that they desire but which make them feel uncomfortable. It is only in these hidden spaces that true growth and expansion can occur.

When you ask these powerful questions, feel into their energy. Watch their facial expression and body language.

Are they afraid to go somewhere? Okay, let's go there. Are they avoiding something? Let's shine a light on it. Let's see if there is a breakthrough that's waiting to rise to the surface.

If it gets to be too much for them, give them space. Take a pause. Wait a moment. Allow them to come back to you after they've explored that thought, idea or emotion in their minds.

Then get right back in.

Asking powerful questions is a skill and a talent. It must be developed over time. It involves understanding language. Expression. Body movement. It is the heart and the soul of extraordinary coaching. Invest in yourself and spend time learning the art of asking powerful questions.

It's one of the best things you can do as a coach.

TOOLS

Master the art of asking powerful questions with these amazing books:

Co-Active Coaching
by Henry Kimsey-house and
Karen Kimsey-House

The Three Dimensional Coaching Program
by Blaine Bartlett.

CHAPTER 16

CRUSH FEAR

> *"Fear doesn't exist anywhere except in the mind."*
>
> -DALE CARNEGIE

It's a paradox. The thing that scares you is the very thing that pushes you further. Higher. Faster.

Think back to a time when you felt afraid.

Maybe it was the first time you were behind the wheel of a car or the time your dad took off the training wheels on your bike. Freedom is right there for the taking. Pure liberation is within your reach.

But then, something happens.

You rev up the engine of that car; you put both feet on the pedals of that bike and that voice, oh, that lovely inner voice takes over.

"What if you hit someone?" "What if you lose control?"
"You've only been doing this for____; you don't know enough!"
"What if you crash into a building?"
"What if you fall and hurt yourself?"

At that moment, that feeling of unadulterated freedom recedes, and it's replaced with intense, paralyzing fear. This fear stops you dead in your tracks. You panic. You get super anxious. A cascade of emotions floods your system, and all you see is a red sign that reads:

C A U T I O N!!!!!
Dangerous, unknown territory ahead!!!!!

We've all experienced some version of this, and it's held us back again and again. Some of us quit the first time we hear that voice. Some of us keep going but the energy and time it takes to overcome our fear squeeze all of the joy and fun from new experiences. It usually gets to a point when you don't want to try anything new anymore.

But there is a solution. A workaround. I've tried it. My friends and clients have tried it.

And it works. Every time.

It's the secret to overcoming fear: Feel that fear run through you and reframe it as enthusiasm.

Call it exhilaration. Think of it as "excitement for the unknown." *"That's not a solution, Ajit. How can reframing fear as excitement work?"* It does and to understand how let's go back to biology class for a minute.

Scientists recently found that the region of the brain that processes feelings of fear also processes feelings of excitement.

The *exact* same region.

When fear is made predictable, our brains process that feeling of fear as excitement.

Think about it...

We love horror movies, and terrifying roller coaster rides because we are certain we will be safe. Our fear is predictable.

What does this mean for you and me and everyone else who has an understanding of how fear and excitement are processed in the brain?

It means you can begin to train your brain and your thinking to reframe fear as the 'excitement for the unknown.'

It means you'll stop feeling afraid and start to feel excited instead. This is huge.

Epic.

Life-changing.

With this awareness of how fear actually works, you can crush fear within yourself and use this methodology to help your clients navigate and overcome their fears.

Let's explore further.

The Freedom Of Choice

We all have stories from our past and meanings attached to these stories. Maybe you almost drowned in a pool as a child, and now, 30 years on, you're too afraid to learn to swim.

Your story = you nearly drowned as a kid.

The meaning you've attached to it = you might die if you learn to swim.

These stories and the meanings we attach to them, give rise to irrational fears. Holding onto fear shuts down the prefrontal cortex in your brain - the region that's responsible for activating creativity and for good decision-making.

Irrational fears push you into an endless spiral of negative thinking, self- doubt, and behaviors to pacify the fear such as overreacting, overeating, overindulging, and full-blown addictions such as workaholism or alcoholism.

This image captures what goes on in your brain during a fearful emotional state:

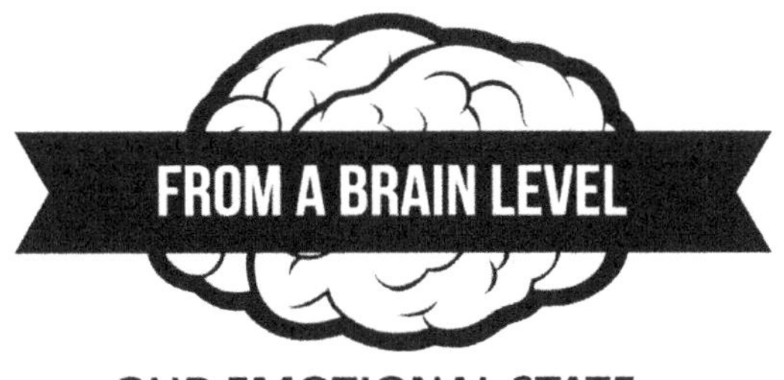

OUR EMOTIONAL STATE...

Sends data to the thalamus, our switchboard...

Arrives at the amygdala (for reactions). If there is a threat...

Automatic sensory response, i.e. stress to the entire body goes off...

Amygdala blocks the slow thinking response to prepare for the anxiety state (flight/fight)

Shuts down the part of our brain involved in creativity, judgment, and decision making. Hence, why our emotions in the presence of "perceived anxiety" or "fear" we enter the process of overreacting, overeating, overindulging—or in other words, engage in behaviors to pacify the cycle.

Image from Emotional GRIT: 8 steps to master your emotions, transform your thoughts, and change your world.

So, let me ask you this:

How does fear show up for you as a coach? Where does fear show up for your clients?

Have you examined how your culture and life experiences shape your identity? How are old fears about life and work and relationships causing you to make bad decisions over and over and over again?

When we choose to be ruled by fear, and when we allow the not-yet- happened to dictate our actions and behaviors, we're giving up the most important freedom we have: the freedom to choose.

Fear Cultures

It takes tremendous courage to chart a different direction from the one we've been on, and fear takes away that courage. Fear limits our thinking and keeps us locked in the past or tied to a dark future that hasn't happened. A future that will probably never happen.

This is why you MUST crush fear and help your clients to do the same.

But before you wage war against fear and win, you must first understand it. This is where fear cultures come in.

Professor Daniel Cordaro, Head of the Yale School of Emotional Intelligence, reports there are 3 Fear Cultures:

3 FEAR CULTURES

CULTURE OF AVERSION

"This isn't enough" so you do whatever it takes to avoid shame.

2 **CULTURE OF SCARCITY**

"There isn't enough" so you become hypercompetitive, over protective/selfish.

3 **UNWORTHINESS**

"I'm not enough" so self-acceptance becomes conditional; failure will happen, since expectations can never be met.

These **Fear Cultures** make up your mode of thinking and are then channeled and expressed through your:

- behaviors
- beliefs
- values

These elements comprise your internal belief systems that you have built up around a specific subject or aspect of your life.

If your grandparents survived the holocaust the 'Culture of Scarcity' is likely to play a central role when it comes to food. They believe there's never enough food. Their value is that food is a priceless commodity. They express all of this through their behavior. For instance, food must never go to waste in their home. No matter what. Even if it means overeating or overindulging.

Building Emotional Resilience

You can crush fear with emotional resilience. It's the only way remove the shackles that prevent you from achieving your optimal potential. Emotional resilience is about establishing inner stability, and this is based on one critical premise – your ability to create and sustain healthy boundaries.

Healthy boundaries are the fundamental component to mastering emotional resilience.

If you're a people-pleaser and you are unable to draw effective and appropriate boundaries around what you're willing to tolerate and what you're not willing to tolerate from others, your emotional stability is non-existent because your emotions are subject to others' whims and wants.

You'll develop deep resentment toward clients, partners, team members and all the other important people in your life. You'll struggle to think clearly and end up with unwanted, negative thoughts in a dark cloud that constantly threatens to consume you.

Setting your terms for healthy boundaries as a coach, and an entrepreneur is pivotal. Without boundaries, you simply cannot survive, let alone thrive. You'll rapidly experience burnout.

Protective Shield

Healthy boundaries are essentially a series of personal rules. They're non-negotiables that protect and honor your deepest values, your energy and your time. They guide you to make the right decisions on what you are willing to consent to and give to others. Most important of all - boundaries define how you wish to lead, serve, and collaborate.

When you have healthy boundaries in place, you'll find a sense of inner balance, and have the energy to pursue your priority goals. You'll start to believe in yourself, develop authentic confidence and understand your best qualities and your limits.

Boundaries work as a protective shield that guards against the demands and expectations, and projections of others that are incongruent with who you are and what you need to do for yourself to function at your highest level.

But most people have weak boundaries, and some have no boundaries at all. This is dangerous and self-destructive.

Here are some common traits and tendencies you'll find in someone with weak boundaries:

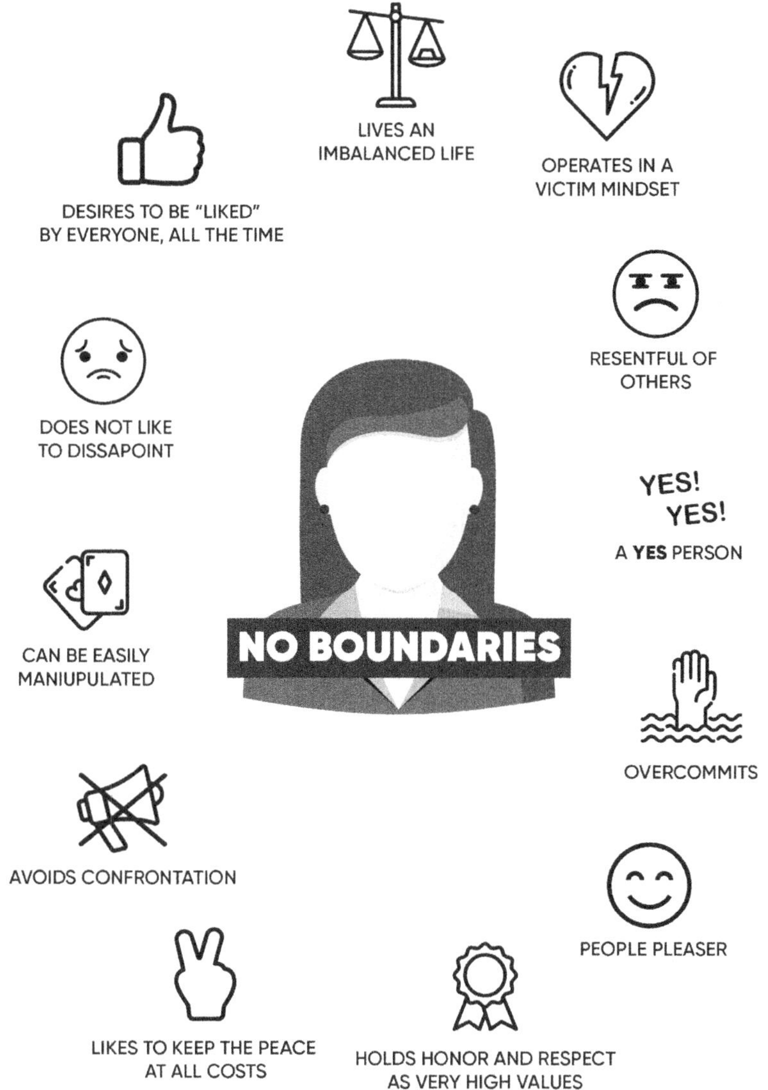

Without healthy boundaries, the following elements become a part of life:

- Ongoing resentment
- Complete burnout
- Constant feelings of fear, guilt and shame

- Anxiety and panic attacks
- Feeling high pressure to perform perfectly
- Stuck and unable to make decisions

Weak boundaries are particularly prominent in parts of the world where cultural expectations and obligations are deeply rooted. If you or your client comes from a family or a communal environment, where there is no sense of 'personal time' or the expectations of the family outweigh your personal wants and needs, you are highly likely to have weak boundaries.

Weak Boundaries in Your Clients

If you're working with a client who has weak boundaries, you'll notice the client overworking, and overdoing everything without any regard for her health, well-being or personal wants and needs.

Keep in mind that your client is unlikely to recognize that she has weak boundaries. Instead, she'll probably call it "hard work" or "climb up the corporate ladder." This usually goes on until she faces complete mental exhaustion or physical health problems.

In her personal life, the client will allow relationships that are toxic and friends who don't respect her time and who take her for granted. Her love life is a series of toxic partners who want her to "prove her love."

These are all negative circumstances but with help from a good coach – that's you – she can learn to take a stand and declare her wants, desires and needs. She can build her life and work based on her own beliefs and values, not someone else's projections.

She can build emotional resilience and set herself free from her fears

Weak Boundaries in You

As a coach, having weak boundaries will allow fear and anxiety to rule everything you do your work and your relationships with clients. It will eventually destroy your practice. This is not an "if" situation. It's a matter of when.

WEAK BOUNDARIES IN YOUR COACHING PRACTICE

	Clients who consistently fail to show up for coaching sessions
	Being afraid to ask for payment or to raise your prices
	Friends/acquaintances who keep asking to "pick your brain" to get free advice
	Clients who don't pay you in full
	Clients who don't pay you at all
	Clients who control your time
	Clients who do not follow through, or drop off in the middle of a coaching package
	Clients you know you can't help but you try to anyway
	Pain-in-the-a** clients you wish you never said YES to
	Overcommitting yourself to too many projects because your're afraid you'll miss out or you're afraid to say no
	Taking on more clients than you have time for
	Clients who hit on your, or who try to start a personal friendship

Cultivating Healthy Boundaries

If you aren't already operating with clear, healthy boundaries, now is the time to start.

Here are the questions you need to ask yourself and your clients:

- What are your highest values and what are the character traits that are important to you? (example: punctuality, honesty, reliability)
- What are some of the behaviors and actions that bother you? What are your pet peeves? (example: people who are rude, critical, dishonest)
- What are you NOT willing to tolerate (example: clients calling you past 8 pm, friends asking for free advice, clients who always pay late, etc.)

Healthy boundaries are a critical aspect of creating results for your clients. It is the most important element in establishing yourself as a service provider for human transformation, and it is a key element in becoming an extraordinary coach.

But keep in mind that setting healthy boundaries – especially if you have never done it before – will be unbelievably challenging. You will be tested every single day. People will push their luck. You will have to uphold your boundaries again and again and again.

My advice?

Keep this chapter of the book marked. Come back to it and read it again and again. It will serve as a reminder that you are on the right track - that it is important for your success and sanity, that you draw the line and create healthy boundaries. Build your "boundary creation muscle." Whatever you do, do NOT fall into the trap of thinking you will disappoint your clients or worse lose your clients.

You will not.

Instead, you will receive a tremendous amount of respect, and enjoy credibility, esteem, and confidence as you attract clients who will receive maximum benefit from your coaching skills. These are the clients who, with your help, will achieve what they set out to do.

Healthy boundaries also give you the strength and capability to effectively grow your business. Boundaries will help you create the right team and create clear expectations with current clients, and future clients.

No more misunderstandings. No more drama. No more wasted time, energy and effort.

Healthy boundaries. It's the secret ingredient to becoming an extraordinary coach...
A coach who crushes fear every day...
And who shows clients how to do the same.

Ask Yourself

1. Which one of the 3 Fear Cultures has played a pivotal role in your life, so far?
2. Can you think of one particular instance where your behavior pattern has caused you to either hire the wrong person, make a bad business decision, or continue to stay in a negative situation?
3. Define your boundaries, your non-negotiables as a coach. For example: what do you tolerate and what are your non-negotiables (punctuality, no calls after 10 pm, no meetings on Fridays): these are your rules, and there's no right or wrong answer.
4. What are 4-6 ways your boundaries can be violated as a coach, and how will you respond to this?
5. Think of a client (future, or current): What are some of the possible outcomes if you were to address your boundaries with this client? Having the awareness and deep understanding of the mindset of where the other person is operating from is key.

6. Self-reflection: How have your personal boundaries being invaded? Do you have feelings of resentment, anger, or stress? Do you feel taken advantage of or as if your relationship is not respectfully mutual?
7. Is there a negative teammate, a demanding family member (mom guilt-trip effect) or a significant other/toxic friend/business partner who always makes you feel guilty? Identify this person and reflect on what you can do to set up healthy boundaries and improve the relationship.

CHAPTER 17

10 PRINCIPLES OF EXTRAORDINARY COACHING

"The greatest gift is not being afraid to question."

-RUBY DEE

When I first started coaching, I went all out. I signed up a bunch of clients, and I jumped straight into serving them. I created loose structures and frameworks for our sessions together.

I discovered very quickly that I had the skills to enroll clients, but I couldn't hold on to them. They didn't come back for more.

In that first year of coaching, not a single client re-enrolled with me. They all seemed to have loved our year together. Their businesses grew. But none of them came back.

I was confused and curious. So, I did what I always do when I don't know what's going on – I started researching. I wanted to know what would get clients to come back again and again.

I knew, instinctively, that I would have to take my coaching skills to a whole new level – an extraordinary level – if I wanted clients lining up to re-enroll with me.

My research revealed some simple but profound truths that I rely on to this day. I developed a potent set of coaching principles based on those truths. I call them 10 Principles of Extraordinary Coaching.

These principles will help you create transformational sessions with clients that will keep them coming back for more.

Again and again and again.

Principle #1 Build Rapport

Your client needs to feel comfortable sharing their deepest fears and challenges with you. You are their supporter and collaborator. You're there to get them to the next level and beyond doing that well, your client MUST trust you. She must connect with you on a deep, emotional level.

And the best way to create that level of trust and connection is to build rapport.

Milton Erickson was a renowned psychiatrist and one of the most skilled hypnotists the world has ever known. Erickson was one of the first to declare that human beings have a conscious and a subconscious mind. He also stated that the subconscious mind is far more powerful than the conscious mind.

And he's right.

Our hearts beat without us thinking about it. We breathe all day, every day of our lives, without having to focus on a single breath. We can hold on to memories of events and experiences that happened years and years ago.

And it's because of the power of our subconscious minds. Milton found that when we connect deeply with someone, we are connecting with them on a subconscious level.

Building rapport creates a subconscious bond that flows outward into the conscious mind.

It's that feeling you get when you've just met someone for the first time, and you think, "I really like this person! It's like we've known each other for years!" That's rapport.

Rapport can happen completely naturally, or you can engineer it. Either way, it works.

The most powerful way to create rapport with someone you've just met is to use a technique called 'mirroring.' Ever noticed how couples who have been together for a long time seem to talk in the same way? They often share similar physical gestures too. This phenomenon can also be detected among close friends, long-term business partners and any duo or group of people who are deeply connected. This is mirroring in action.

Mirroring is one of the fundamental techniques taught in Neuro-Linguistic Programming or NLP - a highly effective communication and personal development tool that's used by some of the world's most successful people including top coaches like Tony Robbins.

It's easy to implement this technique.

You can "mirror" your client by matching their tone of voice, the pace of their breathing, hand gestures, body positioning, and movement. Don't aim for an exact match – this will be obvious and come across as weird and contrived.

Stay casual and gently duplicate their voice, tone, movement, and mannerisms. Do this for just a few minutes, and you'll be amazed at the connection you'll create with your client.

Principle #2 Share Stories

Sharing stories is an effective way to help clients view their challenges or problems from a fresh perspective. Stories gently take your clients out of their current reality and into a new reality. You can use metaphorical stories or experiences that actually happened to you.

Stories are powerful change-makers. Use them generously in your coaching sessions. I personally maintain a stack of stories that I can use to draw context, inspire, question and challenge my clients.

Be mindful that your stories are not outrageous tales or highly personal experiences that create anxiety or discomfort in your clients. It's not about oversharing. It's about helping your clients find inspiration and new insights.

Principle #3 Set Intentions

When you don't set clear intentions at the start of your journey with a new client, you're opening yourself up to all kinds of trouble. It's a simple step, but when you miss it - disaster!

I learned this the hard way.

I've lost big money - hundreds of thousands of dollars - all because I didn't set clear intentions with the client from the get go. Use the following questions to set practical and clear intentions:

- What are the outcomes we are expecting out of this coaching agreement or coaching session?
- What is the vision for our work together here?
- How will we get the results?
- How will we connect and engage during our time together?
- Ask your client: Are you a 100% committed to this coaching experience?
- Ask your client: Are you willing to NOT let your fear get in the way?

When you've discussed these questions, note the answers somewhere so you can refer to them regularly with your client. These intentions will do more than create clear expectations at the start. They will also help you track progress over the long-term. You and your client will be able to see the magic and the results of your work together.

Your client will know that you've been supporting them; how you've helped them in the past, and how you can help them now and in the future. Setting intentions and reminding your clients of these intentions creates a container for trackable, impactful results.

Principle #4 Stay Present

Coaching takes a lot out of us. It drains our energy. It's exhausting. Especially if you've been doing it all day.

All month. All year. Year after year.

Staying present, at all times, when you're doing such a demanding job can be very stressful. It can even feel impossible.

This is why you need rituals that will help you get back into the present moment, again and again. You are doing a disservice to your mission and your client's needs if you allow yourself to drift away.

Create rituals that are right for you and that work with your personality, likes and dislikes. To get you started, here is a list of rituals I personally use when I need to get back into the present moment:

- **Dance**: Dance your ass off to your favorite jam! It will get you to release frustration or anxiety, center you and help you get into a state of flow (see Chapter 3 for more details on achieving a state of flow).
- **Read something powerful**: Mark inspirational phrases or passages in your favorite books to help bring you back to the present.
- **Play music you love, music that inspires you**: This is great for moving your energy and bringing you back to center.
- **Watch something inspiring**: Watch a quick talk, presentation or a section of a movie that you love. This can transform your state in an instant.

- **Meditate:** If meditation is your thing, go somewhere quiet and peace out for a bit.
- **Recap your vision for your future:** If you've written a vision for your future, read it again. If it's in the form of images, look at it for a few minutes. Let it sink in. See yourself getting there. See yourself win.
- **Strike a Power Pose:** I read this in Amy Cuddy's great book called Presence. Amy explains that when you strike a power pose, you'll almost immediately start to feel more confident. Find a power pose that makes you feel strong and powerful and use it whenever you need to.
- **Grin for no reason:** You may feel a little stupid when you first start to do this but keep going. That fake smile will soon translate into real feelings of happiness and pleasure. Try it. You'll know I'm right.

Principle #5 Don't Get Attached

I still get riled up when the techniques, ideas, and insights I share with a client don't work for them, but then I remember this principle and the feeling disappears.

If you notice yourself getting upset or worked up based on a client session, it means you are too attached to your client's outcome.

This is a massive mistake.

As a coach, you can instigate and support the process for change, but you cannot guarantee results.

Period.

Whether a client has a positive outcome or negative outcome, it is their outcome.

You are the facilitator. It's their action, their reaction, their journey, their outcome. Attaching yourself to a client's outcome will hurt the client and affect your energy. When you tie yourself to a client's outcome, you become emotional. Both you and your client will feel excited or sad or frustrated or worried.

As a coach, this level of emotion will stop you from guiding the client in the best possible way. I know it's impossible not to feel any emotions - you are human after all! But do what you need to do to suspend and let go of your emotions as quickly as you can so you can do what you're there to do...

Coach at the highest level.

Always aim to give your client your very best. This means you need to keep your emotions in check. This means you need to let go of your client's outcome.

Principle #6 Be You

This may seem obvious, but it needs to be said...

When a client decides to work with you, they have decided to work with you.

Not someone else. Not someone you're pretending to be. So, bring your WHOLE self to the table.

You are made up of your experiences, your learnings, your teachings. Make sure you bring all of real you into your coaching sessions.

No holding back. No pretending. No excuses.

Principle #7 Be Brave

I first heard the term "Fearless Coaching" when I read The Prosperous Coach.

The concept captured my attention and it stayed with me. Fearless coaching is what I aim to do in every session with a client. I currently work with leaders, and many of them are entrepreneurs. Almost all of them are more financially successful than I am and they are also older than I am.

It's easy to feel intimidated and to let my fears guide my coaching sessions.

But I follow this principle every moment of each session with a client - no matter how wealthy they are, how experienced, how accomplished and how impressive.

Being brave in your coaching allows you to ask questions that you would otherwise be hesitant to ask. When you let fear guide you, you lock down your mind and allow your doubt to sabotage what you can do for a client.

To me, the word brave allows me to experience the fear of asking a question and go down that rabbit hole anyway. It makes room for caution, but it also encourages me to ask the question anyway.

Be brave. You will do yourself and your clients a huge favor.

Principle #8 It's Not About You...

...or about what you think is right.

It's not about your systems and strategies or how good you are at what you do. None of it is about you. Check your ego.

It's about the *client*.

Their dreams. Their challenges. Their beliefs. Their lives.

You are there to serve them. You are there to help them. Never forget that.

Principle #9 Don't Judge

Let me give it to you straight...

Sooner or later, your client is going to make choices or do something you feel is wrong. You will naturally feel like making a judgment about who they are and what they stand for.

It's important to understand that what we believe to be right or wrong, good or bad is based on our personal experience of this world. Our beliefs are not neutral. They are biased and connected to our views, our background, upbringing, level of exposure to other cultures and thousands of other elements.

So, keep your views in check. Your client is coming to you and sharing openly with you because they trust that you will not judge. This is an unspoken rule of coaching.

Don't judge.

Principle #10 Don't Make Ass-umptions

Ass-umptions. That's what they are.

When we make an assumption, you are making an ass of yourself and of the person you are coaching.

So, don't do it. If you are not clear, ask "Would you clarify what you mean by this?".

If you are clear, ask anyway "Could you elaborate on what that means?"

When you avoid assumptions, you achieve 2 things.

First, you will always know exactly what your client means. Second, you encourage your client to go deep and explain how they think and feel about a situation or experience.

When you keep asking question – without making assumptions - you aren't just making things clear for yourself, you're making things clear for them.

Sometimes, these simple questions will open a whole new conversation and allow your client to see new ideas or truths that they didn't even know existed.

Ask Yourself

How can I use the 10 Principles of Extraordinary Coaching in my sessions with clients? Which principles will I put into practice right away? Here they are again for reference:

1. Build Rapport
2. Share Stories
3. Set Intentions
4. Stay Present
5. Don't Get Attached
6. Be You
7. Be Brave
8. It's NOT About You
9. Don't Judge
10. Don't make Ass-umptions

10 PRINCIPLES OF
EXTRAORDINARY COACHING
1
BUILD RAPPORT
2
SHARE STORIES
3
SET INTENTIONS
4
STAY PRESENT
5
DON'T GET ATTACHED
6
BE YOU
7
BE BRAVE
8
IT'S NOT ABOUT YOU
9
DON'T JUDGE
10
DON'T MAKE ASS-UMPTIONS

CHAPTER 18

THE GRID OF UPGRADES

> *"Live as if you were to die tomorrow. Learn as if you were to live forever."*
>
> -Mahatma Gandhi

I'm going to come clean.

The coaching principles in the previous chapter are awesome but to rely on just these insights and strategies to enroll clients, and then coach them to create amazing results?

That would be a mistake.

Have guidelines and principles as a reference but always be open to learning new skills as a coach.

The more you learn, the more skills you gain, the more clients you'll change.
The more lives you'll improve.
The more success you'll achieve.
The more impact you'll have on the world.

Expanding your coaching skills must be at the top of your priority list and the "Grid of Upgrades" will help track your progress.

Using the grid is easy. The idea is to choose 3 to 4 new coaching skills to focus on, every year. Make sure you pick at least 1 coaching skill that is outside your area of focus or niche. For instance, if you are a business coach, your external skill could be something that has to do with health.

Once you've decided on the skills, you're going to be learning, look at the grid and write "yes" on the boxes that correspond to the method you'll to use to expand on that skill each month.

At the end of the year, your grid may look something like this:

Month	Skill	Book	Program	Certifica-tion	Seminar
January	Leadership	Yes			
February	Leadership		Yes		
March	Leadership				Yes
April	Body			Yes	
May	Body			Yes	
June	Body			Yes	
July	Team		Yes		
August	Team		Yes		
September	Team	Yes			
October	Presentation	Yes			
November	Presentation	Yes			
December	Presentation	Yes			

The Grid of Upgrades is a simple but effective way for you to hold yourself accountable so you continue to grow and expand your coaching skills and the methodologies you use in your sessions.

When you do this, you'll find yourself growing more and more confident in your ability to create results for your clients.

It's how the world's best coaches operate. It's the mark of an extraordinary

TOOL

Here's a fresh Grid of Upgrades you can use to expand your coaching skills and methodologies. Keep it handy so you can fill it up as you move through the year.

Month	Skill	Book	Program	Certification	Seminar
January					
February					
March					
April					
May					
June					
July					
August					
September					
October					
November					
December					

CHAPTER 19

TOOLS TO CREATE RESULTS FIRST

Programs That Create Results

- Impacting Leaders by Michael Neill
  http://www.evercoach.com/impacting-leaders
- Unleashed by Christine Hassler
  http://www.evercoach.com/unleashed
- Three Dimensional Coaching Program
  http://www.evercoach.com/three-dimensional-coaching

Books That Create Results

- Emotional GRIT by Neeta Bhushan
  http://bit.ly/EmotionalGrit
- Expectation Hangover by Christine Hassler
  http://bit.ly/ExpectationH
- The Inside-Out Revolution by Michael Neill
  http://insideoutrevolution.com/
- Supercoach by Michael Neill
  http://bit.ly/Supercoach-Neill
- Prison Break by Jason Goldberg
  http://bit.ly/JG-Prison-Break
- The Code of the Extraordinary Mind by Vishen Lakhiani
  www.thecodexmind.com

BECOMING ABUNDANT

CHAPTER 20

BECOMING ABUNDANT

> *"The key to abundance is meeting limited circumstances with unlimited thoughts."*
>
> \- MARIANNE WILLIAMSON

"How do I become a successful coach?" "How do I grow a 6-figure practice?" "How do I get to 7 figures?" "My business has been stuck at the current size for quite a while. How do I grow it?"

These are some of the most common questions I receive and when you break them down and get to the core, every one of them centers on a single theme: becoming abundant.

Coaches who are serious about what they do want to become successful. They want to know how to create an incredibly profitable business and this is as it should be.

But when they ask me about it, I give them the same short answer. Be brave. Have structure.
When I tell them this, they're often surprised. What has becoming abundant have to do with being brave and having structure?

Another short answer… Everything.

Being Brave

This is one of the 10 Principles of Extraordinary Coaching (see Chapter 17) and it applies strongly in your path to becoming an abundant coach.

You simply cannot build a successful coaching practice when you are weighed down by doubt and fear.

Being brave is about not thinking too little of yourself. It's about you doing those things you need to do even when fear is paramount. Even when you feel frozen. Even when you want to run and hide.

Why do we fear so much? Why do we trust so little? What's at stake? Truly at stake?

For decades, other people – parents, teachers, bosses – consciously and unconsciously gave you the message that you're not good enough.

That nothing you do is ever good enough. That you need someone else to validate you and your accomplishments. That you need a piece of paper to prove your worth. And your skills. Your value. And your genius.

Let me tell you something extremely important…

Certifications and degrees – there's nothing inherently wrong with them. More power to you if you have them. If you want some sort of traditional paper qualification, go ahead and get it. If you receive praise and approval from others because you have them, go ahead and enjoy all of it.

But know this.

A piece of paper will *not* transform you into a good coach. It certainly won't turn you into an extraordinary coach. It will not get you clients and it will not give you the magical ability to answer all questions. Heck, it won't even help you create consistent results for clients.

Some of the best *coaches I know are not certified. Some of the smartest most qualified coaches I know, are not successful.*

Coaching powerfully and building a massively successful coaching practice has *nothing* to do with validation from the world. It has nothing to do with "*studying*" to become a coach.

A group of researchers conducted a study on what it takes to become a success. They followed the lives of a number of high school valedictorians to find out if these high achievers would go on to live incredibly successful lives.

The results were surprising. They found that most of these high achievers in high school ended up with average careers. Even more shocking - some of the "low ranking" students who just scraped by, became outrageously successful.

Never tie your success to your qualifications. Get certified to give yourself some comfort. Get that degree because you want to learn more. But coach because you enjoy it. Because it challenges you. Because it allows you to be creative. Because it allows you to be yourself.

Don't coach to save the world. Don't coach to save your client. And don't coach to save yourself. To prove your worth. To show that you're important and successful.

If you do, you're being way too serious and your clients will feel the energy and weight of your aspirations. Don't put the weight of "being a successful coach" on them. It's not fair and it sucks the joy out of the entire experience.

Instead, let them enjoy it. Support them with what they need. Be brave with your coaching. Don't judge them. Don't judge yourself.

Love deeply. Express openly. Play freely.

Be brave with yourself. Be brave with your clients.

Don't let your desire to be an "extraordinary coach" hold you back. Let this desire become your wings so you can fly.

The truth is you are already an extraordinary coach. You don't have to try to become one.

You are an extraordinary coach because you are an extraordinary human being. I know you won't settle for anything less that your best. You know you won't settle for anything less than your best.

Allow this truth to set you free so you can be brave. So you can enjoy the experience. So you can become abundant.

Structure

Another element of starting and growing a successful, prosperous coaching practice is structure.

I know what you're thinking. Structure is restriction. Confinement. It's a box.

We don't want to be boxed in. Nobody does. But here's the thing...

A box is a structure, but a structure doesn't have to be a box.

I have had tremendous amount of freedom for the past few years of my life. I don't have to report to anyone. I make enough money to do what I want to do, buy what I feel like buying and splurge when I want to.

When I first experienced this level of freedom, I found it to be quite a challenge. I realized, with shock and amazement, that...

Freedom to do anything, makes you want to do nothing.

I found that when you have all the freedom in the world... It becomes boring. It makes you feel anxious. It's meh.

My conclusion? True freedom isn't about doing nothing or doing everything.

True freedom is about choice.

The choice to have focus in your life. To welcome challenges. To have crazy highs and stressful lows. To have godly adventures. To feel scared, just a little. To laugh a lot.

True freedom can only happen when you have the choice to create the structure you want in your life.

Structure is power. Structure gives you purpose in your business. Structure is also not limited to freedom.

It's everywhere. And it should be everywhere. It doesn't have to be a restriction.

Structure fuels freedom. True freedom.

Ask Yourself

Why do I want to coach? What do I really want to experience? If I created an ideal day, how would it unfold? What does true freedom look like to me?

CHAPTER 21

SELLING IS LOVE

> *"Here is a simple but powerful rule ... always give people more than they expect to get."*
>
> -NELSON BOSWELL

Selling is love.

This is not just a catchy title; it's the essence of how sales should happen. How sales must happen. When selling is about love, it's easy.

Never sleazy.

But for most coaches selling is the big, "scary" monster they must conquer. It's the work they don't want to do. Entire books have been written about sales and selling. Some of the best-selling programs for coaches are all about sales but, despite all of this help and support, selling is still the biggest problem for most coaches.

Shift Your Energy

Most sales training and programs focus on techniques. Techniques are great. They are useful. They are helpful when you are a beginner. It gives you a framework to follow.

But techniques can rapidly get old. They quickly become stale. Certain sales techniques can feel incongruent with your values.

We are not going to dive into sales techniques here. That would add another 15,000 words to this book! Instead, let's reframe how you approach sales.

Let's shift your energy around selling. It's the fastest, most effective way to boost your results.

Service. First. Love. Always

When we hear the word "sales," when we think of selling, we think of used car salesmen. Or pushy men and women distributing product samples on the street. You might envision people like those guys in the movie The Wolf of Wall Street.

We don't think doctors sell. We don't think teachers sell. We don't think most of the coaches we love and admire sell. For some reason, their images don't pop up in our minds when we think of sales.

But let me tell you this - nothing happens in this world unless someone sells something to someone else.

An entrepreneur needs to sell the benefits of a world-changing invention to get funded. Mother Teresa sold her message to help the poor, sick and needy in India. The Dalai Lama is selling peace and joy.

These types of sales don't seem icky, tired, or pushy because they were made with love.

Sales expresses who you are as a coach to your potential client. It's an expression of what is possible when you show up in their lives and serve them powerfully. When you coach them, so their lives change and become better.

What do you think about when you think about selling? Is your inner dialogue, "How do I get them to buy?" or is it "How can I help them create the changes they want to create? What is the support they need?" When you ask the last 2 questions, your energy and viewpoint changes. Your conversation moves from "need" to "service."

When you ask, "How do I get them to buy" you need them to sign up. You are thinking of sales strategies. You are stuck inside your mind. You are not listening to the potential client. You are blocking honest communication.

When you are in the place of service, all you're doing is serving. When you are serving, you are listening consciously. You are communicating authentically.

In 1971, Albert Meridian published a book called, *Silent Messages*, where he presented his research on nonverbal communication.

He found that prospects based their assessments of credibility on factors other than the sales person's words. The prospects assigned 55 percent of credibility to body language and another 38 percent to the tone of voice. They assigned only 7 percent of the sales person's credibility to the actual words that were spoken.

This means prospects trusted the sales person's gestures, body movement and the sound of their voice over their words.

When you come from a place of service you will automatically send a very different message via your nonverbal communication.

You will communicate authenticity. You will communicate respect.

Sell from a place of service. Sell from a place of love and all of the other pieces will fall into place.

Getting to A "Hell, Yes!"

As humans, we don't want to be rejected. We want to be loved. We want to accepted. We want to be recognized.

When we get a NO from our clients after a sales conversation, it feels like the world is falling apart.

We start thinking about that no.

We wonder if we're good enough? We wonder why they said no even though we offered our service with our heart and soul.

This can be demotivating. Even depressing. I have met coaches who do an outstanding job at selling someone else's coaching products and packages but when it comes to their own, they freeze.

This happened to me.

A few years ago, I had a unique opportunity to get on stage and deliver a talk to 40 kickass coaches. I was supposed to make a sales offer after the talk but when the time came, I froze. I kept talking about everything else, but that offer.

I started the Q&A session.

I let the session go on and on to avoid making the offer.

I did manage to get up the courage to do it, but it was at the very last possible moment.

I made the offer in the last 10 mins of a 180-minute presentation.

During the weekend that led up to that presentation, I had completed 40 coaching sessions.

40, 60-minute 1 on 1 sessions in one weekend.

It was 10 to 12 grueling hours of coaching over 4 short days.

I started at 8 in the morning and continued coaching until 8 at night. My result? I enrolled 4 clients.

40 individuals had expressed excitement to work with me, but after my presentation, 36 of them said "no."

A few of them came close to a yes but ended on a firm "NO". That's 36 strong no-s and 4 yes-es.

That's a 90% rejection rate.

I learned two lessons that day.

First, that's how it works. You have to find that "yes" between many "no- s." Over time my yes: no ratio went from 1:9 to 1:3. I get a yes for every 3 sales conversations I have.

My personal yes rate improved because of many factors. I became comfortable with my offer. I learned to come from a place of service. I learned how to make my offer to the right clients.

The second lesson happened a few months after that presentation from hell. I had received a no, from one of the individuals at that event. A few months later, he showed up at another event. We talked. I had no intention to sell or to try to enroll him into a coaching package. I already knew he was not interested. He had given me a clear "no" at the earlier event.

But soon after we met for the second time, I received an email. He wanted to know if the coaching package I had offered, at the event where we first met, was still available.

That "no" became a "yes." Or as Rich Litvin says, it became a "hell, yes!" This experience taught me my second lesson. No is not always a no.

Sometimes - many times - it might just be a "not right now."

TOOLS

#1 I know you might be thinking, "How do I sell with love?" "How can I get comfortable with enrollment conversations?" Lindsay Wilson, is a respected master coach and sales trainer. Selling with love - that's her zone of genius. She shares her expert insights on this topic in an awesome, free online training. Go to this link http://www.evercoach.com/ booked/online-training/ invite

#2 I'd also like you to check out Mindvalley's Jason Campbell. He gave an awesome take on selling with love called 'Why Selling is the Greatest Expression of Love.' Go to this link: http://bit.ly/SellWithLove

CHAPTER 22

CLIENTS ARE EVERYWHERE

"It is only through seeking that we find what we are looking for."

-SETH ADAM SMITH

"Where do I find clients? Is there a secret place where clients hide?"

I was talking to world class life coach Christina Berkley about finding clients. I asked her those questions, and without missing a beat, she gave me my answer, *"Clients are everywhere."*

I instantly recognized the truth in those 3 simple words. Christina went on to tell a story that showed me she walked her talk.

She was on a fairly long flight from one end of the U.S. to the other. There was a gentleman seated next to her, and they started talking. Turns out, he was a senior executive at a major corporation. He shared a few challenges he was having at work. With permission, Christina started coaching him. When the plane landed, they traded contact details.

The very next day, he reached out and hired her.

Christina had found a client without even trying. This is a great story, and it illustrates Christina's point perfectly - clients are everywhere.

So, let me ask you this... Are you looking?

Become a Client Magnet

I found my first client at a live event and my second client at a different event. My third client came from my email list. The fourth from a weekend seminar where I had been invited to speak.
It feels incredibly complicated at first but becoming a client magnet isn't hard when you know how. Here are a 5 simple but effective client attraction techniques that I personally use. They work really well.

#1 Attend events that your clients love

Go to events you know your clients will love. If you are a life coach go to seminars designed for people who want to change their lives. If you are a health coach, attend health-related weekend workshops, and events.

#2 Attend industry events

Attending industry events allows you to meet other coaches, and collaborate. You might even form a partnership that fuels your business. I know of a partnership between 2 coaches, who are experts in different but related niches. They consistently trade high-end clients with one another. It's a match made in heaven.

#3 Share your message regularly

Use social media platforms, podcasts, YouTube videos or any other social channel to share your message. What you have to say is important, and when you share it with the world, the right clients will find you. Don't let fear hold you back. Be brave.

#4 Speak at events

Speak at as many live events as you can and don't just pick the ones with big audiences. I started speaking at seminars with 10 people in the audience. Every person counts. 5 people. 3 people. Give them your best. Then do another event. Keep going, keep speaking, keep moving forward.

#5 Write a powerful proposal and hit send

Write a 4-page document that expresses who you are. Talk about the challenges your clients face. Explain why they have these challenges. Describe new possibilities and bigger opportunities. At the end of the proposal, make an offer to have a conversation. Reach out to your potential clients via LinkedIn, Facebook or any other platform and send the proposal via email. Then, serve powerfully when you have a chance to have that proposed conversation. Demonstrate what it would be like to work with you as their coach.

Clients are everywhere. You just need to look.

Ask Yourself

Where can I find my clients? Where will my clients go to learn, improve, get help and find solutions for their biggest challenges? Who can I speak with to generate more opportunities to create clients? Who would make a great partner to trade clients with?

CHAPTER 23

THE POWER OF PRE-SELL

> *"People don't care how much you know until they know how much you care."*
>
> -THEODORE ROOSEVELT

I have a client. Let's call him Justin. He's a big-name speaker. He's also a dear friend. A go-getter. During a coaching session, we discovered one of his biggest challenges – consistency.

Consistent revenue comes from consistent client interest. Justin was having some trouble retaining client interest.

In his best-selling book, *Influence,* Robert Cialdini discusses the concept of social proof. When other people talk about a product, service, or person, we are more likely to trust that product or service, or person. This is social proof.

We used this concept with Justin. We started with these questions...

What if your clients connected with you before they ever engaged you as a coach? What if your clients noticed their friends talking about you before they actually noticed you on their own? What if your clients saw you all over Facebook before they even found out what you do?

It worked.

After weeks of testing and trying and finding what to tweak to get Justin in front of his clients, we finally created a powerful ecosystem of clients. He now generates between $200,000 to $300,000 every month in coaching and consulting sales.

Now when clients get on the phone, they are already excited about Justin. They want to figure out how to work with him. They already know, Justin is a powerhouse coach.

They are pre-sold on the idea of working with him.

Not About Sales

Pre-selling takes away the need to establish authority. Pre-selling takes away the pressure of communicating your values and beliefs to your clients. Pre-selling helps you get straight to the results you want.

You can pre-sell with your videos on Facebook. You can pre-sell with your articles on powerful blog platforms such as Medium. You can pre- sell with your posts on LinkedIn.

Pre-selling is mostly about creating authority on channels where your clients like to hang out. If they are on LinkedIn, you can pre-sell by writing posts for LinkedIn on subjects that matter to your clients. If they are on Facebook, you can do the same by creating content, Livestreams, and videos and sharing these with them.

You may be thinking, *"If I pre-sell before they even know who I am, wouldn't potential clients feel annoyed. Maybe even pissed off?"*

They won't because pre-selling to your clients is not about sales. It's about connecting and creating an authentic, emotional bond.

Creating That Connection

Religion and politics. These are 2 areas that create a powerful emotional reaction in people.

Why is that so?

One way to look at it is that a religious organization or political party expounds very clear, specific beliefs. The people who join these groups believe in the same things. They wouldn't join otherwise.

The same thing happens in friendships. Except there is one more emotion that kicks in - *care.*

If we can represent our values and beliefs and relay it back to our clients, while showing how much we truly care, we can create an almost unbreakable sense of connection and trust.

Keep in mind that once you go down this path, once you decide that you're going to be open about your beliefs and values to support your message, you risk alienating some people but this is more than okay. These people would have never become your clients, anyway.

Know this: if you are brave and vocal about your beliefs and values, you *will* attract clients who are aligned with you and who are on the same wavelength.

Clients who are looking for a coach who "gets" them. A coach who is authentic. Someone they can relate to... Someone who shares their values and beliefs. Someone like you.

TOOLS

List your personal values and beliefs in the left column, below. In the right column, list the values and beliefs that you stand against.

Values and Beliefs (Stand For)	Values and Beliefs (Stand Against)

As you list your values and beliefs, you will realize that your best clients are aligned with what you stand for.

Once you have these values and beliefs listed, go ahead and make a video or write a post about every one of them.

Do the same for the ones you are against.

Sharing what you believe in and what you stand for allows clients to find that resonance with you, even before they hit your website. Even before they speak with you. Even before you have a sales conversation.

Sharing your beliefs will attract clients you'll love. And clients who'll love you in return.

CHAPTER 24

BRAND...YOU

> *"Life isn't about finding yourself. Life is about creating yourself."*
>
> -George Bernard Shaw

In the coaching business and even in the teaching business, it all comes back to you.

Who are you? Why do you do what you do? What do you represent?

If you want hide who you truly are, if you're afraid of stepping out and being visible, you're in the wrong business. If you want your clients to say, "She's the best in the business," or "His track record speaks for him," or "You should talk to her. She's the expert!" you need to clearly convey your personal brand.

Most coaches believe personal branding can be put off until much later in the game, but the truth is you need to start creating your brand pretty much after you sign your first client.

Speak. Write. Coach.

So how do you convey your brand?

Speak. Write. Coach.

You can do it for free. For small payments. For 10 mins. For 3 hours. It doesn't matter.

I talked to a celebrity speaker about her journey. She is a mentor of mine. Here's what she said:

"Ajit, when the recession hit in 2008, most of the speakers out there, were charging their usual rate to get on stage. None of them reduced their fees. None of them understood the long game.

I, on the other hand, changed my approach. I asked the event producers, what they could afford. Even if it meant slashing my fee in half, I would take it. It wasn't about the money. It was about being there when people needed me most.

And because I was there, when the others were not, now when these companies are doing great they are happy to hire me for more than I would ever think of charging.

That's how it all started for me.

People get too attached to speaking fees, and what's in it for them. I just went for it. I would speak on a stage with an audience of 10 people. 20 people. 200 people. I would speak for free. I would speak for a small fee.

My only intention was to build my name. My reputation."

This woman is now a sought-after speaker. She regularly books 6-figure speaking gigs around the world.

Her brand and her reputation are flawless and how did she get there? She spoke. She wrote. She coached.

Show Up

Speak wherever you can.

On a stage. A podcast. A weekend workshop. If you're not speaking at live events, go to Facebook or Instagram or LinkedIn Turn those platforms into your personal stage. Just make sure you speak

Write whenever you can.

Write a book. Write an article. Write a blog post. Write a social media message. Just make sure you write.

Coach whenever you can.

Coach for free. Coach for a small fee. Coach for short term package. Just make sure you coach.

Every single interaction you have, adds to your personal brand. Every time you show up with power, passion, and purpose, it adds to your personal brand.

Master coach Christine Hassler once told me about her podcast, and how she shows up and coaches there. That podcast not only got her clients, but it also got her a TV show.

Christine shows up. She coaches.

I was at a Tony Robbins seminar. He shared the story of how when he first started, he would go to Venice beach in LA and coach anyone who was willing to get coached.

He showed up. He coached. For free. Speak. Write. Coach.

Convey your personal brand. Whenever you can. Wherever you can. Brand, YOU.

TOOLS

Consistently coming up with ideas to write, speak, coach and spread your message - that can be overwhelming. I get that. That's why I created a free online training where I share specific strategies you can easily implement to create content magic on a consistent basis. Follow this link to know more:
https://www.evercoach.com/first- serve/online-training/invite

CHAPTER 25

GOING BIG

"Life's too short to think small."

-TIM FERRISS

There is an upside and a downside when you take your coaching practice into the digital world.

The Downside:
Nonstop distraction and noise.
Lower quality communication.
Confusion and complication.
Digital connections reduce high-touch engagement and the possibility of connecting with high-end clientele.

The Upside:
Greater reach.
The ability to pre-sell and brand quickly – this compresses the sales cycle.
Ease of creating multiple channels of engagement like live online talks, books, programs.
Higher revenue in less time.
Passive, potentially consistent, income.

Yes, there are 2 sides. But the upside outweighs the downside. Especially when you want to go big.

Massive Audience

Using online media channels takes time, resources and investment. This means when you start your digital journey; things are going to get mega stressful. Ultra-strenuous.

But over time, you'll see the rewards.

One caveat: if you want to serve only high-end clients, you can skip digital. High-end clients like high-touch connections, so you're better off connecting with them at live events, meetups, workshops, and seminars. But if you want to have a major impact on a high number of clients, if you want to reach a massive audience, going digital is the answer.

Write that ebook. Create that online coaching program. Start a membership site with fresh, monthly content.

There are countless powerful, effective ways to connect and spread your message online. But this is a plus point that can turn on you pretty quick.

Here's what I mean...

Just One

Coaches quickly get overwhelmed with digital platforms because they think they need to be everywhere and do everything. At all times. They must tweet, and post social media messages and write blog posts for LinkedIn.

Not true.

If you want to build a million-dollar coaching practice, focus on one digital platform. If you want to get to 3 million dollars, focus on one digital platform. 5 million? Still one.

You only need to start thinking of more than one platform when you cross over to 8 or 10 million dollars, but most of us don't even want to mess around with those kinds of numbers. We'd be happy generating $250,000 in profits.

Heck, a $100,000 would be awesome!

If this is you, don't waste your time, energy, money and effort trying to master every, single digital platform out there. Just pick one and do a kick ass job with it. Communicate effectively. Powerfully. Consistently.

Start by making a list of topics that you want to talk about or write about every day in your chosen digital channel. Think engagement. Think value. You can even reuse the same content every couple of months. When it's powerful, when it's thoughtful, when it's useful, your clients won't mind seeing it again.

They'll even thank you for the reminder.

As for you...

You'll get what you set out to do. You'll show them you care. You'll spread your message. You'll share value. You'll engage, consistently. Powerfully. And you'll go big.

Ask Yourself

What is your preferred digital channel to share your message? What are five powerful ideas that you have a lot of knowledge about and want to share with others? What are 2 different ways that you can present the same idea to your audience in a creative way? What is stopping you from sharing your content with others today?

CHAPTER 26

PERFECT PRICING

I'm always looking for a new challenge. There are a lot of mountains to climb out there. When I run out of mountains, I'll build a new one."

-SYLVESTER STALLONE

It's time to focus on a common challenge just about every coach deals with sooner or later - pricing.

So, where are you at right now? Where do you want to be?

$200 per hour? $300 per hour? $500 per hour? Are you breaking out into a sweat, yet?

Let's keep pushing those numbers up. How about $700 per hour? $800 per hour? How about $1000 per hour?

Check in with yourself. What's the number that gets you feeling really, really uncomfortable? Write that down. What's your per hour rate right now? Write that down too. Pick a number between where you are and the number that made you uncomfortable.

That's your challenge. That's your sweet spot. Let's get to that. How about you make the next 10 proposals with your new number?

I know, it's scary, but it's also exciting, no? As soon as you start to get comfortable with your new number, move it up by 10% or 20%.

Keep it challenging. Keep it moving.

My first coaching package was for $15,000 per year. It's at $70,000 per year right now. It went up to $100,000 per year for a brief moment. I didn't feel comfortable with that, so I brought it back down. That's ok too.

A coach and a friend, let's call her Dawn, told me she was charging $250 per hour. We brainstormed. We decided she would not position her offering on a "per hour" basis. It would be for 3 or 6-month coaching packages. These packages would be calculated at $350 per hour. This worked out to $2,800 for 8 sessions over 3 months or $5,600 for 16 sessions over 6 months.

She lost one client. She gained three new ones. She also gained confidence and certainty. She could focus on the actual coaching. Upleveling her number was challenging for Dawn. A little scary, and very exciting.

What's your sweet spot? Your magic number? That price point that falls exactly between scary and exciting. That's your perfect price.

Pick that. Show yourself you can get it done. Let that be your challenge.

You can also choose another related area to challenge yourself - client enrollment.

Who are you enrolling right now? Friends? Friends of friends? Distant cousins? How about we take that up a notch? How about approaching strangers at an event? Does that feel little scary but exciting?

Then go for it.

When you get a no, let it mean: "Not right now." When you get a yes, let it mean: "That's a great start!" Don't settle. Challenge yourself a little. And when you're ready, challenge yourself a lot.

Don't feel like you have to restrict your challenges and focus on just pricing or client enrollment.

Challenges makes us braver, as coaches. Stronger. Smarter. More resilient.

So go ahead and explore. Make it a game. Have fun. Create abundance. Freedom. Adventure. Learn. Grow. Change. Expand.

This is why we play the game… The game of coaching.
The game of life.

TOOLS

Below is your "Challenge Yourself" grid. In the column marked Challenge, write the challenges you want to take on (one of these challenges should be around raising your prices/rates and another should be about enrolling clients) Add a date beside each challenge. Under "yes" write the meaning of it. Under "No" write a meaning for it. Under purpose, repeatedly write why you do what you do.

Let's do 10 yes-s on our challenge first. And then, let's up it! Go for 20, 30 and more!

Challenge	Yes	No	Purpose

CHAPTER 27

HOW CAN WE WORK TOGETHER?

> *"It is literally true that you can succeed best and quickest by helping others to succeed."*
>
> -Napoleon Hill

You had an enrollment conversation with a potential client, and she said the words you love to hear. It's like music to your ears.

"How can we work together?"

Ladies and gentleman, we have a winner! But that feeling of euphoria dies down quickly. You realize what you say next could make or break that powerful connection with this client. The connection you worked so hard to build throughout the conversation.

So, how do you answer that question without screwing things up? Without losing the client?

First, don't jump to the price right away. You want to show them what's possible before you talk about your prices. If you lead with the price, it leads to a comparison with other similar services, or they'll compare against how much services in other categories cost per hour.

So, first, talk about the results they'll achieve when they work with you and how you will get them there.

This is about painting a word picture of how they will feel, and what they will experience when they get to the place they see in their minds. That dazzling future. Those daring goals - achieved. Share stories and examples so they can visualize, feel, and imagine what it would be like to work with you.

When you've created a clear word picture, it's time for the second step.

Numbers

Don't go into the conversation unprepared. Know your coaching packages, know your prices, inside out. When you know all of this, and you know what you can help them create in their lives, the transformations you can bring, the new beginnings that will happen, you will show up with confidence.

And they will experience the impact you will have on their lives when they work with you.

That's when they'll enroll. That's when they'll sign up. That's when the adventure begins.

Define Your Coaching Packages

It's absolutely vital that you define your coaching packages. This definition must include types of coaching as well as the potential revenue you would like to generate.

Start defining your packages by getting clear on the various ways clients can work with you.

1 on 1. Workshops.
Digital Programs.
Retreats.
Seminars.
Intensives.

You don't need to offer all of these, just the ones that you enjoy and your clients love.

In my case, there are only 3 ways to work with me. You either do a one-to-one for a year.
You do a 1 or 2-day intensive. Or you can join my mastermind.

That is all.

I personally define my coaching packages, using a Coaching Package Grid. It gives me a clear understanding on the types of coaching arrangements I'm going to offer plus my revenue or income. Here's an example:

Type of Coaching	Available Slots	Per Person	Charge
One on One Coaching	2	20,000	40,000
Intensives	9	5,000	45,000
Group Coaching	10	2,000	20,000
		Total	105,000

I already know that in a year I want to have 30 active coaching days. On the other days, I like to work on my other businesses, like Evercoach. This helps me decide on the types of coaching and what I need to charge.

Having a limited number of active coaching days also helps me understand how many enrollment conversations and free coaching sessions I need to have to hit my desired revenue.

It shows me how much active selling I need to do. And when I can stop.

Another benefit? When you define your coaching packages, it helps your clients understand that you are available for a limited number of days, in a limited number of ways.

This may sound like a bad thing, but it's not. Limited choices help people make accurate decisions. Fewer choices make it easy for them to select how they want to work with you.

Can't afford 1 on 1 coaching? Join the group program. Don't want to do something that's spread out over a year? Pick the intensive. You quickly start to see how your clients like to work with you.

For me, intensives won the race. My clients love when I come in for intensives, every 6 months. I work with them for 2 days straight, and they walk away with solid action steps and strategies they can implement immediately in their business.

It's powerful for them. It's powerful for me.
How can you get awesome results for your clients? What are they asking for from you? What is the easiest sale for you?

Answer those questions and you'll easily define coaching packages that you and your clients love and that create a consistent revenue stream that supports your lifestyle.

TOOLS

#1 Take as much time as you need to fill the following Coaching Package Grid. If you're just starting out and you've never had a client, use the Grid to get clear on what you would like your coaching packages to look like. There is no right or and wrong here. It is your practice. You get to decide. But decide something. It will give your clients clarity and give you confidence and income.

Type of Coaching	Available Slots	Per Person	Charge
One on One Coaching			
Intensives			
Group Coaching			
Retreat			
Digital Programs			
Digital Live Programs			
Workshops			
		Potential Revenue	

#2 The administrative details of a coaching package such as client contracts or what you can and cannot include in different types of packages is beyond the scope of this book. We partnered up with world class life coach Christina Berkley to create a program that can help you navigate this terrain. The program is called Elements.

Click here or follow this link http://www.evercoach.com/elements/online-training/invite

CHAPTER 28

COACH, COACH, COACH

> *"It is always the simple that produces the marvelous."*
>
> -Amelia Barr

You're a coach. That part's obvious.

But how do you build a business around that?

That part's actually easier than you think. And it's profound. You coach. Then you coach some more. And you keep coaching. Coach. Coach. Coach.

I'm not trying to be glib. I'm being honest. Your aim should be to coach someone every, single, day. Immerse yourself in helping others Don't let not-so-good results stop you. Don't let great results go to your head. Just keep coaching whether you're successful or not.

I coached a client who couldn't afford my rate. I did it for free. He didn't sign up but what he did do was so much better. He talked about me to his friends. He shared the coaching experience he had with me, with his clients. His colleagues. His family members.

Connections and introductions were made. Good things came out of these. Partnerships and affiliations that I could not have imagined or engineered on my own.

I carried on coaching for free until I found a paying client. And another one and another one.

A coach, coaches.
A great coach coaches often. An extraordinary coach coaches all the freaking time.

This method works. It's worked for me. It works for countless other coaches. Friends have introduced me to coaches because they had an amazing experience. I have hired many of these people based on recommendations alone.

There is no better way to let clients know what you can do. What you can accomplish. Don't tell them. Show them.

By coaching. The more you show them, the more they get to experience your skills.

This greatly increases the likelihood they'll work with you. If not now. Then one day.

I can hear, my friend Rich Litvin, and author of *The Prosperous Coach* say in his distinct British accent, "Coach your ass off!"

Rich is one of the most successful and respected coaches in the world. He has built his entire practice, by coaching his ass off. His clients love him. They know he generates results. They trust him to create transformations. And he delivers. Without fail. They've experienced it for themselves.

If you do nothing else with this book if you try nothing.
If you experiment with none of the ideas I've shared so far, at least do this:

Coach. Coach. Coach.

The Ideal Client Tracker

I generally like working with two categories of business owners. Businesses generating over 1 million in sales.

Extraordinary individuals who are in transition.

I'm always on the lookout for potential clients in these categories and when I meet them, I get their contact information and set that aside.

When I'm in enrollment mode, I list all the potential clients I would like to work with in the IDEAL CLIENT TRACKER, using my contact information, I reach out to them during my "enrollment season" via email, Facebook or text.

Then, I schedule a conversation. I serve them. I immerse them in a coaching experience. If I they're ready to take massive action, I propose a way to work together, on the call. If I feel they're not ready yet, I suggest a follow-up.

That's my personal formula. It's based on the same central premise. The one that never fails.

Coach. Coach. Coach.

TOOL

Here's the Ideal Client Tracker. Go ahead and start to use it to capture a list of ideal clients you can connect with when you're ready to enroll.

Who do I want to coach?	Response to reach out?	Coaching Call Scheduled	Coaching Call Follow Up	Proposed Package	Yes/No

CHAPTER 29

TOOLS TO BECOME ABUNDANT

"Any fool can know. The point is to understand."

-Albert Einstein

Programs That Create Abundance:

Booked by Lindsay Wilson:
http://www.evercoach.com/booked

Amplify by Franziska Iseli:
http://www.evercoach.com/amplify

First: Serve by Ajit Nawalkha:
http://www.evercoach.com/first-serve

Personal Brand Power by Marisa Murgatroyd:
http://www.evercoach.com/personal-brand-power

Elements by Christina Berkley:
http://www.evercoach.com/elements

Book That Create Abundance:

The Prosperous Coach by Rich Litvin and Steve Chandler:
http://www.evercoach.com/the-prosperous-coach

Free Resources:

Abundant Coach by Ajit Nawalkha:
http://www.evercoach.com/extraordinary-coach

Online Workshop to learn Effortless, Heart-Centered Sales Methodology:
http://www.evercoach.com/booked/online-training/invite

Online Training for Learn How to Run Workshops and Masterminds:
http://www.evercoach.com/amplify/online-training/invite

Online Workshop to Learn How to Package Your Services
http://www.evercoach.com/elements/online-training/invite

9 Proven Strategies to Communicate Your Message Online
https://www.evercoach.com/first-serve/online-training/invite

DO

CHAPTER 30

DO

> *"The way to get started is to quit talking and begin doing."*
>
> -Walt Disney

Do.

It's the mantra that has kept me going. It's the mantra that has kept most successful coaches and entrepreneurs going.

It's the simplest strategy there is, and it will get you that win you're looking for, every time.

Do.

Don't allow yourself to be limited by what other people tell you.

Don't allow yourself to be limited by what I tell you. When you decided to become a coach, you took an important step. A step many people don't have the courage to take. So, don't let anyone stop you now.

When you feel, you don't have the right skills or that you don't know enough, think back to the beginning when you felt lost, uncertain and afraid. You figured it out then. You've figured it out again and again since then. Know that you'll figure it out every time.

Then keep moving forward.

If it starts to get complicated, break it down, let it sink in. Then keep moving forward.

If it gets scary, remember that you've failed gloriously and you're still here. Remember how it didn't matter in the end. How you made progress anyway.

Then keep moving forward.

If everything starts to feel overwhelming, and frustrating, tear down those big goals, and rebuild them on small step at a time.

Then keep moving forward.

No one has control over your life but you. No one can tell you what's right for you but you. No one gets to define who you are but you.

Know yourself. Then keep moving forward.

Do.

But Do It Right

Do does not mean "being busy." It means taking focused action that moves you forward.

Don't let your fears hold you back. Don't let your past hold you back. Break the shackles of fear that keep locked inside a prison in your mind. Then keep moving forward.

Do something that scares you. Something you know will create forward movement.

And while you're doing that something, keep these rules of success in your mind. We've talked about them in previous chapters, but I want to share them here in this simple, easy-to-refer list:

- Seek extraordinary clients. Allow them to experience your genius.
- Enjoy the journey. If you're just starting, understand you're the new kid in the game – and be ok with that.
- Do everything from a place of service and love.
- Remember relationships are built over time – often a "no" just means "not right now."
- "Yes" from a client is just the beginning. Seek to "wow" to "fascinate" to "blow their minds."

Never forget...

You are amazing. You are creative. You are extraordinary. There is no reason for you to feel "less than" or to play small.

Step up. Shine on.

When in doubt, reflect on how far you've come. Stand tall. Feel proud and...

Do.

Do because you want it. Do because you love it. Do because you enjoy it.

Doing something - even when things are messy, even when you're filled with uncertainty - creates momentum.

Momentum creates progress. Progress will give you more confidence. More focus. More direction.

This will help you do even more. This will get you to your goals. Your dreams. Your vision.

Do.

It's the best way. It's the only way.

CHAPTER 31

STAGES OF SUCCESS

"Your life will be no better than the plans you make and the action you take. You are the architect and builder of your own life, fortune, and destiny."

- ALFRED A. MONTAPERT

As we get closer to the end of this book, I want to leave you with a strategy that will give you a little more certainty, a little more comfort, as you head toward becoming an extraordinary coach.

This is something you can do yourself. Something that will inspire and motivate progress. Something that will make the journey easier.

Below is the map of your entire journey to success, abundance and freedom, marked out in stages. The journey doesn't always flow in exactly the same way, but it does follow this general direction.

As you move from one stage to another, here are a few pointers that will help you know where you are, and what you must prioritize.

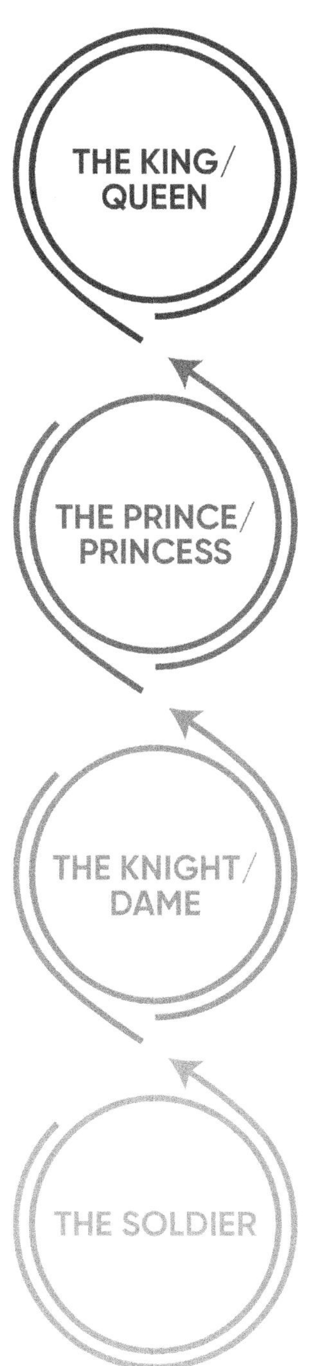

Stage I: The Soldier

This is the stage when you first get introduced to coaching. You like the idea. You're inspired to know more, so you start to educate yourself on the subject.

At this stage, you'll probably juggle part-time part time coaching as you hold down a full time or part time job somewhere, to pay the bills.

You'll have some basic understanding about coaching in, or you'll have some experience in the field, but you are still a newbie. Still learning the ropes.

If you're a soldier:

- You'll make very little or no income from coaching. Your numbers will be well below $10,000 a year.
- You'll have another job
- You spend a lot of time observing what other coaches are doing
- You're not sure about your next step
- You spend way too much time on social media, commenting on or reading other people's posts
- You feel awkward when you're coaching someone, and you feel downright uncomfortable making sales calls

If you're a soldier, you should:

- Coach as much as you can even if you have to do it for free. Money isn't the focus at this stage. It's about gaining experience.
- Learn coaching methodologies. Talk about coaching with others. Test and explore your methods with friends, colleagues and family members
- Focus on building confidence in yourself and in your ability to make an irresistible offer to people you meet.
- Start going to events that will help you understand and master the art of running a successful coaching practice
- Start going to events you know your clients will love so you can meet them, connect with them and get to know them

Stage II: The Knight/Dame

At Stage II, you're starting to feel confident as a coach, and you even have a few clients.

If you're a Knight/Dame:

- You have some income coming in from coaching – between $10,000 and $50,000 a year
- You have a handful of clients
- You have started thinking about creating coaching packages
- You overwhelmed by how much you have to do to grow your coaching practice

If you're a Knight/Dame, you should:

- Start creating coaching packages
- Spend a lot of your time conducting coaching conversations
- Find ways to get comfortable with rejection. Look for the yes's, between the no's
- Start going to industry events so you can become a better coach.

- Start going to industry events to learn about creating coaching packaging and mastering sales

Stage III: Prince/Princesses

At this stage, your client list has grown, exponentially. You've gained traction, and you're successful. But this is also the stage where you'll start to feel stuck.

If you're a Prince/Princess:

- You've been coaching for 2 to 5 years
- Your income is great- around the $200,000 mark per year.
- You have a ton of clients
- You're working way too hard.
- You catch yourself wondering, how you're ever going to grow with so much on my plate
- You start to value time more than money

If you're a Prince/Princess, you should:

- Pay very close attention to your prices. Price is paramount right now. Consider increasing your prices by 10%, 20% or 30%
- Hire a team to help with the sales process so you can have more time and energy
- Hire a coach who can support you at this stage
- Start improving your online presence as you create online programs
- Think about writing a book to increase your credibility as an authority in your area of expertise
- Focus on increasing enrollment rates to your mastermind or group coaching program.

Stage IV: King/Queen

The fourth and final state is when you get to experience more stability in your business. You are looking to make a bigger impact and increase your reach. You want to be part of high-level masterminds and find a community of kindred spirits who understand you, your challenges and your vision.

If you're a King/Queen:

- You're hitting $500,000 to $1,000,000 or more per year.
- You have a solid online presence.
- You are selling digital programs, and books
- You host 1 or 2 annual events that support your group coaching and 1-on-1 coaching programs
- You may even have some junior coaches who are part of your team
- You have a sales team
- You want to know what's next
- You are often frustrated with your pace of growth, and team issues take up most of your time.

If you're a King/Queen, you should:

- Focus on improving your team management and leadership skills
- Put together systems and processes to optimize team performance
- Create more channels to promote yourself, your products and services
- Upgrade your website. At this stage, your website is your calling card.
- Recreate your vision. Make it bigger and more exciting. Something that will pull you forward
- Get a coach who can help you scale and who understands your work and your unique situation
- Keep in mind that hyper-growth at this stage can kill your business.

The 4 Stages of Success are not the only way to grow your coaching business, but I've found this pattern to be the most consistent.

Keep these stages and challenges in mind, then design your own adventure.

CHAPTER 32

THE FIRST 60 DAYS

> *"A year from now you'll wish you had started today."*
>
> -KAREN LAMB

As a coach and consultant, I literally can't sleep at night unless every one of my clients walks away with clear action steps they can implement right away.

I feel the same way about this book and you, dear reader.

In this book, we explored the 3 critical elements for extraordinary coaching– You, Your Methodology and Your Business. It's the only framework you need to create a transformative and extraordinary coaching business.

Before we end our journey together on these pages, I want to leave you with a powerful way to DO something that will move as you forward. This is something that will allow you to take a step-by-step, gamified approach towards enrolling clients and making an awesome impact in your life, your business and your clients.

Like all of the other methodologies, tasks, and actions outlined in this book, this last one is simple but incredibly effective.

Ready for it?

All you need to do is mark your progress toward becoming extraordinary.

Do it every day, for the next 60 days. It will revolutionize your business.

It will transform how you see yourself. It will change your whole life.

Guaranteed.

At the end of 60 days, you'll achieve more goals than you ever thought possible. You'll start to generate income through your coaching – or create far more income than you already have. You'll attract and enroll amazing clients. You'll change lives. You'll have an impact. You'll begin to achieve that level of excellence that you've been dreaming of. And you'll do what you set out to do...

Become an extraordinary coach with an extraordinary business.

TOOL

Use the grid below to list out 60 action items for the next 60 days. Make sure every one of these action items will help you move forward. Choose actions that can be completed within a day or less. These actions should be based on the stage you are at in the Stages of Success (see Chapter 31).

Before you start taking action, review all items on your list. Check in with yourself during the review process. Become aware of how you feel in your body when you think about each one.

Do you feel excited and open to it or does it feel wrong and incongruent? Feel into your 60-day game plan and make adjustments based on the stage you are at and the results you want to create.

I want to acknowledge two coaches who do this exercise really well: Rich Litvin with the 90-day Money Game and Christina Berkley with Hatch and The 5K Project.

We are proud to have both of them as authors and teachers at Evercoach.

Week	Day	Action	Progress/Notes
Week 1	1		
	2		
	3		
	4		
	5		
	6	Planning Day	
	7	Rest Day	
Week 2	8		
	9		
	10		
	11		
	12		
	13	Planning Day	
	14	Rest Day	
Week 3	15		
	16		
	17		
	18		
	19		
	20		
	21	Planning Day	
	22	Rest Day	
Week 4	23		
	24		
	25		
	26		
	27		
	28		
	29	Planning Day	
	30	Rest Day	

Week	Day	Action	Progress/Notes
Week 5	1		
	2		
	3		
	4		
	5		
	6	Planning Day	
	7	Rest Day	
Week 6	8		
	9		
	10		
	11		
	12		
	13	Planning Day	
	14	Rest Day	
Week 7	15		
	16		
	17		
	18		
	19		
	20		
	21	Planning Day	
	22	Rest Day	
Week 8	23		
	24		
	25		
	26		
	27		
	28		
	29	Planning Day	
	30	Rest Day	

THE BOOK OF COACHING ONLINE EXPERIENCE

This book comes with a *free* online course!

This means you'll have unlimited access to hours of additional in depth, high-value training, practices, and content designed to help you fully absorb and implement the insights, techniques, systems, and ideas you've discovered in these pages.

For instance, if you want to know more about a specific concept from one of the coaches I've highlighted in the book - such as Michael Neill - the course will give you deeper insights and understanding when you listen to my full interview with him.

This unique Online Experience also includes awesome extras such as gorgeous images, photos, and videos plus it's all easily available on the web and on Android, and iOS.

When you dive into The Book of Coaching Online Experience, you'll have free access to:

- Actionable, transformational training for coaches that's designed to create real world results.
- Additional strategies and proven techniques to rapidly up-level all aspects of your coaching practice.
- Tasks and exercises to skyrocket your personal and professional growth.
- A dynamic, interactive community of like-minded coaches who will share your journey and give you the support you need ... and SO much more!

Access The Book of Coaching Online Experience here:
www.evercoach.com/the-book-of-coaching/tools

Special Invite:
Mindvalley Masters Community

Calling all coaches, transformational teachers, authors, experts, impact makers and anyone with a burning desire to change the world...

We'd love for you to join a growing tribe of rockstars just like you!

Become part of our private Mindvalley Masters Community here:

https://www.facebook.com/groups/mindvalleymasterscommunity/

The secret password is "Mastery" ;).

Acknowledgements

This book would have remained an idea in my mind if not for the love, guidance, and support of so many amazing people in my life...

To my beautiful co-creator and magic maker, Neeta. You are a brilliant, powerful coach, my inspiration, and my rock. Thank you for always being there for me and for being a patient partner throughout the course of writing this book. Without you, The Book of Coaching would not exist.

To Vishen Lakhiani, out there, you may be known as my business partner, but in my heart, you are my brother. Your crazy vision has created a massive tidal wave of revolutionary ideas that are transforming the way the world lives, works and plays. Thank you for being one heck of a partner. Without you, this dream of mine would not be a reality.

To the team at Evercoach by Mindvalley: I want to celebrate every one of you. Your incredible talent and gifts have brought my vision to life.

To Alina, for keeping us all in check, for bringing some much-needed sanity to our crazy world and for always giving us a warm, wonderful smile even when stress levels hit the roof.

To Siddharth, for dreaming big, and for juggling the unknown and known with equal efficiency.

To Ana Sofia, for your creativity, and dedication and for that loud Latina flavor that never fails to brighten our days.

To Brian, for being the extraordinary wordsmith that you are and for your marvelous sense of humor. Thank you for your burning ambition and for always believing that we can do more, and be more.

To Francesca, for being at least 2 steps ahead of the curve, for your drive, your dedication and for letting us know why no Latina should ever go to Vipassana :).

To Shantini, our editor, for capturing the essence and wisdom of a swirl of words from two different writers, for helping us communicate our knowledge and insights with clarity and especially for understanding and updating my "flowery" English :).

To all the authors at Evercoach by Mindvalley: Rich Litvin, Jason Goldberg, Christina Berkley, Christine Hassler, Marisa Murgatroyd, Lindsay Wilson, Marisa Peer, Franziska Iseli, Jessica Nazarali, Michael Neill, Blaine Bartlett, Bryan Franklin, Jennifer Russell, Michael Drew, and Sam Cawthorn. I want you to know that you are the reason we are now the largest platform for transformational teachers. Thank you for your genius, your generosity and for joining hearts and hands with us to elevate and empower people around the world.

To our gifted designers Raydi, Krysta and Jason for your amazing talent and for creating the stunning, impactful designs here.

A special shout out to everyone at Epic, especially Himanshu, for flawlessly bringing all of the technology pieces together.

To the team at Mindvalley, whose motivation, talent, and boundless belief made Evercoach happen.

To my beloved family...

My parents, Ashok and Chandrakala, my brother and his wife, Atul, and Siddhi and my nephews, Avish and Aarush. To my in-laws Santosh and Uncle Glenn and Neeta's brother, Vinay. You keep us going every day. You are our inspiration, our life's mission and the reason we do what we do. Every one of you will live in my heart forever.

And last but not least, to you the extraordinary, heart-centered coach. Thank you for choosing this book. Thank you for wanting to grow and expand. Thank you for being you. Coaches like you are changing lives. Coaches like you are changing the world.

Serve, first.
Love, always.

Ajit
August 2017

Resources

A-Fest: www.Afest.com

Marisa Peer at A-Fest "The Biggest Disease Affecting Humanity: I'm Not Enough": http://bit.ly/Iamenough

Cal Newport and Deep Work Book: http://bit.ly/Deep-Work

Daniel Pink, Drive: https://www.amazon.com/Drive-Surprising-Truth-About- Motivates/dp/1594484805/

Mihaly Csikszentmihalyi, Flow: https://www.amazon.com/dp/0061339202/

Dan Pink, Ted Talk, The Puzzle of Motivation: https://www.youtube.com/ watch?v=rrkrvAUbU9Y

Malcom Gladwell and the 10,000 hour rule: http://www.businessinsider.com/new-study-destroys-malcolm-gladwells-10000- rule-2014-7

Prison Break by Jason Goldberg: https://www.amazon.com/B01LP09K5O

Jason Goldberg at Evercoach Summit Live: http://bit.ly/Self-Leadership

Vishen Lakhiani, Code of the Extraordinary Mind: http://www.thecodexmind. com/

Goal Setting Redefined: http://www.mindvalley.com/goal-setting-redefined

Lifebook: http://mylifebook.com/

Jeffrey Allen and Energy Secrets for Exceptional Communication and Connection: http://bit.ly/JeffreyAllen

Dave Asprey, Head Strong: https://www.bulletproof.com/head-strong-book

Vishen Lakhiani and Dave Asprey http://bit.ly/Biohacking-Dave

Intermittent fasting https://www.nerdfitness.com/blog/a-beginners-guide-to-intermittent-fasting/

High Performance Brain
https://blog.bulletproof.com/eat-fat-for-high-performance-brain/

Bulletproof Diet
https://blog.bulletproof.com/wp-content/uploads/2014/01/ Bulletproof-Diet-Infographic-Vector.pdf

Inside Tracker https://www.insidetracker.com/

Dr. Mark Hyman www.drhyman.com

Dr. Mercola www.mercola.com

Dr. Axe https://draxe.com/chia-seeds-benefits-side-effects/

Dance Party Music: http://bit.ly/dance-party-spotify

Electronic Chill Music: http://bit.ly/electronic-chill-spotify

Deep Focus Music: http://bit.ly/deep-focus-spotify

Guide to meditation:
http://bit.ly/Mindfulness-Benefits

Devi Prayer. http://bit.ly/DeviPrayer

Meditation music for your personal mantras:
https://www.youtube.com/ watch?v=Zpf6Nz-MVE0

Holotropic Breathwork:
https://ultraculture.org/blog/2016/02/16/holotropic- breathwork/

Modal Health Show: http://theshawnstevensonmodel.com/podcasts/

This is Your Life: https://michaelhyatt.com/thisisyourlife

Entrepreneur On Fire: https://www.eofire.com/itunes

Shawn Achor, Happiness Advantage:
https://www.amazon.com/dp/0307591549

Emotional GRIT: http://bit.ly/EmotionalGrit

Evercoach Playlist: https://open.spotify.com/user/1297983653/playlist/2TZCTBJdp0RAt0OgPvzt2y

6-phase meditation: http://bit.ly/6Phase

Achiever's Method: www.ajitnawalkha.com/achiever

Coach like the rain, Michael Neill: http://bit.ly/CoachLikeRain

Michael Neill: https://www.michaelneill.org/

Maslow's Hierarchy of Needs:
https://www.psychologytoday.com/blog/hide- and-seek/201205/our-hierarchy-needs

Daniel Goleman: http://www.danielgoleman.info/

Three Dimensional Coaching:
https://www.amazon.com/dp/B00EFELGVO

The Prosperous Coach: www.evercoach.com/the-prosperous-coach

Co-Active Coaching:
https://www.amazon.com/dp/1857885678

Daniel Cordero: http://ei.yale.edu/person/daniel-cordaro-ph-d/

Milton Erickson: https://en.wikipedia.org/wiki/Milton_H._Erickson

Impacting Leaders: http://www.evercoach.com/impacting-leaders

Unleashed: http://www.evercoach.com/unleashed

Three Dimensional Coaching Program:
http://www.evercoach.com/three- dimensional-coaching

Expectation Hangover by Christine Hassler:
https://www.amazon.com/dp/1608683842/

Inside Out Revolution:
http://insideoutrevolution.com/ Supercoach: http://bit.ly/Supercoach-Neill

Silent Messages:
https://www.amazon.com/dp/0534000592/

Rich Litvin: http://richlitvin.com/hello/

Steve Chandler: http://www.stevechandler.com/index.html

Robert Cialdini:
https://www.amazon.com/dp/006124189X

Lisa Nichols: https://www.motivatingthemasses.com/

Tony Robbins: https://www.tonyrobbins.com/

Booked by Lindsay Wilson: http://www.evercoach.com/booked

Amplify by Franziska Iseli: http://www.evercoach.com/amplify

First: Serve by Ajit Nawalkha: http://www.evercoach.com/first-serve

Personal Brand Power by Marisa Murgatroyd:
http://www.evercoach.com/ personal-brand-power

Elements by Christina Berkley: http://www.evercoach.com/elements

The Prosperous Coach by Rich Litvin and Steve Chandler:
http://www.evercoach.com/the-prosperous-coach

Abundant Coach by Ajit Nawalkha:
http://www.evercoach.com/extraordinary-coach

Online Workshop to learn Effortless, Heart-Centered Sales Methodology: http://www.evercoach.com/booked/online-training/invite

Online Training for Learn How to Run Workshops and Masterminds:
http://www.evercoach.com/amplify/online-training/invite

Online Workshop to Learn How to Package Your Services
http://www.evercoach.com/elements/online-training/invite

9 Proven Strategies to Communicate Your Message Online
https://www.evercoach.com/first-serve/online-training/invite

Made in the USA
Monee, IL
11 September 2019